CATCHING DAWN

CATCHING DAWN

A Search for a Dog and the Discovery of Family

MELISSA ARMSTRONG

LANTERN PUBLISHING & MEDIA • BROOKLYN, NY

2020
Lantern Publishing & Media
128 Second Place
Brooklyn, NY 11231
www.lanternpm.org

Cover Design: Abigail Stellpflug

Printed in the United States of America

Library of Congress Cataloging-in-Publication information is available
upon request.

Every word of this book is dedicated to Miss Annie Daisy Banana Fanny Armstrong, the dog with a name fit for royalty and my first unconditional love.

Contents

Acknowledgments

Every time I think about the fact this book is getting published, a symphony of emotions sounds inside of me. Most of all, I feel grateful.

I'm most grateful for dogs. The healing power of their unconditional love inspired this whole memoir. I owe a special thank you to the ones who passed—Miss Annie, Joe Poop, Dessie, Lucy, and Dawn—and to our current pack, Floyd, Sara, Meadow, and Adriana. I'm so grateful for all the mutts we had the opportunity to foster, with a special shout-out to Pippi, Tory, Rosie, the Magic 8, and Tony Soprano.

Thank you Martin Rowe and Lantern Publishing for believing in this memoir and for your patience through this whole process. I'm grateful that I found a publisher who cares about animals as much as I do.

I couldn't have saved a single dog on Sycamore Street or finished a single page of this book if it wasn't for Mason Armstrong. I love you, Mace. It's that simple. I also have to bow down to Donna Wilkins, an activist who never stops fighting for the animals in her rural community.

I owe a huge debt to all the people who played a part in Dawn's story: Lino Chavez, Nancy Padfield, Charlotte Padfield, Dan Hitch, Barbara Jamison, Todd Langston, Geoff Reed, and Dr. Lewis.

I also want to give a shout-out to my biggest cheerleaders, Ruth Laitila, Honora Gabriel, and my brother-from-another-mother Jason Pidgeon. I'm very grateful to Lauren Adams, Hayley Armstrong, Camille Armstrong, and Todd Veney for helping with the dirty details.

I need to thank the Vermont College of Fine Arts and its wonderful writing program. I especially owe a debt to Sue Silverman who helped me cobble together the very first drafts of this memoir. I'm also grateful for the wise counsel of Larry Sutin, Doug Glover, Abby Frucht, and Connie May Fowler.

No single person can save every homeless dog, but a community can make a huge dent. I owe a tail-thumping thank you to the Springfield Animal Control and their officers, who offered their time and resources. I also owe a huge thank you to every single person on Sycamore Street who helped us catch Dawn. Not only did they help save her life, they also helped save nineteen more.

Note: I have changed some of the names of individuals and places and altered some physical details to protect the anonymity of some people mentioned in this book.

PART 1

1

Night

Twenty-four paws drummed on asphalt. Every mutt wore metal identification tags that jingled in rhythm with their stride. The dogs held their slick noses high, picking up as many scents as each of their three hundred million scent glands could hold. Occasionally, a smell overwhelmed one or the other, and they skimmed their snouts over the ground for as long as our speed allowed. My husband, Mason, and I were walking a pack of six dogs at the Springfield Greenway on a June afternoon. We had seven canines with us, but Miss Annie rode in a papoose strapped on my husband's chest. She only weighed six pounds.

Foot traffic was busier than normal on the bridges because of a county-sanctioned free-fishing weekend. People sitting on coolers, folding chairs, and blankets lined the banks of the Sulphur Fork Creek. Fishing lines dangled in the air. Red, blue, and green bobbers speckled the water's leisurely moving surface. By far, most people commented on Miss Annie, our Yorkshire terrier, who was perched on her rear with her front paws hanging on the papoose. She had walked a mile earlier, then plopped down in the middle of the pavement. It was her way of letting us know she'd exercised enough. Annie felt me watching her and turned. We held each other's gaze. We checked in on one another, a brief moment of eye contact, a second of reassurance, a hundred times a day.

A middle-aged woman who wore the aged look of hard living approached us on the bridge near the old waterworks plant. Her skin was an orange-brown, as though she spent hours in a tanning bed.

"Y'all dog walkers?" she asked. She abruptly reached for Miss Annie, and Annie ducked into the pouch. Besides being adorable, my terrier was a snob.

I explained we volunteered for a Robertson County rescue agency called Free Love. Her eyes widened. They were an aquamarine blue, the prettiest feature in a face lined with deep grooves. Her hair ended in a frizzy bob. She pulled it back with a headband decorated in polka dots. It looked like a child's accessory.

"Y'all help folks here in town?" She sounded southern, gruff; a full-time smoker's voice.

"In Robertson County," I answered.

"My name is Bernice Lee, and that there's Tray," she said, pointing to a man sitting on a lawn chair. He wore an eye patch and a do-rag with the American flag printed on it. His foot, propped on a bucket, was wrapped in a cast. It was a lot to take in at once, but even in those first seconds, from the way they talked to the way they dressed, the Lees wore the unmistakable sheen of poverty.

"I got a litter of newborn puppies in my backyard nobody wants," she said. "I thought about calling animal control, but they ain't worth nothing."

I perked up as soon as I heard the word *puppies*. Mason often accused me of being puppy-stupid, meaning anytime one was near I lost all common sense. Beyond their cuteness, intoxicating breath, and cuddling abilities, I loved watching them play. Chestnuts, dandelions, ants, sticks, pine cones, and worms fascinated them for hours. Dogs in general, but especially puppies confirmed my fundamental belief that happiness is found in simplicity.

"I'm pretty sure Free Love can help," I said.

Mason's gaze burned into the back of my skull. I had no idea if Joan Pryor, the nonprofit's head honcho, would be willing to help or not. Joan was a seventy-year-old southern belle with a melodic voice and a backbone of steel. More often than not, when I called her about the strays running up and down our country roads, she couldn't do much more than listen. Free Love existed on six thousand dollars a year.

"One thing," Bernice said. "I don't want you taking those puppies until you catch the momma. I call her Night," she said.

"We've caught strays before," I answered, but that wasn't completely true. Mason and I had picked up homeless dogs sitting on the roadside numerous times, but we'd never chased one who didn't want to be caught. There's a big difference between the two, but back then I didn't understand that.

"Did those strays let you touch them? Cause Night don't let nobody touch her," Bernice warned.

"I promise we'll catch her," I said, but her warning barely registered. Instead, I acted as puppy-stupid as Mason claimed. I told Bernice that catching Night wouldn't be a problem because I was bewitched with images of newborn puppies. I didn't know, couldn't have known, that a simple promise made with the best intentions would embed itself in my life until catching Night was all that mattered.

* * *

Until we met Bernice, our afternoon had been as normal as any other that summer. We were walking dogs and worrying about our elderly mutt Joe. In our house, walking was a ritual. My husband and I took the dogs out twice a day, once in the morning, then again before dark. We piled all seven in two separate cars, both Hondas, and drove to the greenway. We made two trips out of necessity. The closest sidewalks were in Springfield, Tennessee, a small farming city ten miles east. A year ago, we would have brought Joe, but he couldn't manage a few steps anymore, let alone miles.

Mason and I taught the pack to move beside or slightly behind us but never in front. I had once interviewed a dog behaviorist for a blog I wrote about fostering homeless animals. Todd Langston said that taking charge when migrating establishes leadership quicker than any other training method because it taps into dogs' pack instincts. Our daily walks also wore them out. After years of living with more dogs than people, Mason and I believed in the old adage, "A tired dog is a good dog."

For the first couple of miles, I lost my thoughts in the simple act of walking and didn't think about Joe. Two of the mutts we brought were foster animals. They had been living at our house for several weeks, so they understood leash etiquette. The others were family and professional walkers. We moved so harmoniously it seemed as if we glided above the pavement. This shared movement fused us in a space where words didn't intrude, where communication existed outside of language. Dogs are masters at utilizing their senses, at being present in each moment, and on our walks, I emulated them.

In places, the path swerved away from the creek and cut through crops that rotated between hay, tobacco, corn, and soybeans. Buds sprouted through the fields in organized rows, sewing seams of pale green against the dirt. A rain-drenched earth scented the air. A distant coal train rumbled along railroad tracks, and the sound blended with the chirp and hum of numerous birds and insects in the fields. It created a melody as original as mutts, breeds melded with breeds until they were as unique as artwork, each one a masterpiece.

Somewhere around the second mile marker, the sounds of the greenway and the exhilarating feeling of walking in harmony with dogs disintegrated. Mason needed to talk about Joe. Joe suffered from old age and an autoimmune disease. My husband didn't share his feelings often, but the uncertainty that surrounded losing a dog we loved like a child was too enormous to hold inside for long.

Mason didn't look at me when he described how *bad* the morning had been. If I didn't hear his voice catch on the word *bad*, I might not have realized he was upset. That he'd probably been thinking about Joe for our whole walk. That morning Mason had carried him to the front yard to go to the bathroom. Joe wobbled two steps, lost his balance, and did a faceplant. He lay sprawled in the dirt until Mason propped him back up on all fours. It was a humbling and jarring moment, one of the rare times when Mason had admitted euthanizing him *might be* compassionate after all.

There were periods over the last few months when Joe had stopped moving and eating, and we discussed the dreaded topic of euthanizing him. Each time he rebounded and that fact only complicated our decision. At some point, we tried using his tail as our barometer. We would schedule a visit to our vet, Dr. Dan Hitch, when Joe stopped wagging it, but no matter how lethargic Joe became it thumped every time we walked in the room.

The idea that life would continue when he was gone terrified both of us. What would happen to our family after Joe? Would we change? And if so, *how* would we change? Every conversation about euthanizing him ended with a bargain or a justification for putting it off. Our discussion that afternoon ended the same way. Right before we met Bernice, we had agreed to call Dr. Dan if Joe couldn't walk the three yards from his dog bed to the water bowl by morning.

* * *

Bernice flicked her cigarette butt into the creek. Miss Annie finally relented and allowed the woman to stroke her silky hair. Bernice smiled as though touching Annie was an honor. It was a look I saw a lot over Miss Annie's life. The summer before we had stood on the sidewalk as a Labor Day parade meandered through town. When a pink-and-purple-bedazzled float carrying a squad of middle school cheerleaders saw Miss Annie, they pointed and sang a chorus of "ahhhhhhhhh's" so synchronized it seemed as though it had been choreographed. At fourteen, Miss Annie was missing a few teeth. She had cataracts. But she was still in relatively good health. I expected her to live for another two, maybe three years. I'd have time after Joe died. I'd have time to absorb one loss before experiencing another.

"I ain't seen them all yet, but I think Night had eight puppies," Bernice said.

Eight lives just budding instead of ending. Eight lives on the opposite end of existence as Joe. If we caught Night, I could see eight clumsy, curious, silly puppies every day. Nothing would cheer me up more.

Later that evening, I asked Mason, "How hard can it be to trap a nursing mutt?"

For the next six months, it was the hardest thing in the world.

2

Sycamore Street

Mason drove with one hand on the steering wheel and one hanging out the window. We were on our way to Sycamore Street with a bag of Kibbles 'n Bits in the trunk. We didn't know if we'd meet Night, but I planned on cuddling a puppy or two. Occasionally, Mason steered with his knee, as though driving was so easy he didn't need hands. He was a natural driver, the one who always took the wheel. He came by his talents honestly. His father had raced a super gas car. Mason once admitted if he won the lottery, he'd drag race a nitro funny car. My husband was thirty-nine, six feet tall, and lanky, with scruff starting to gray. Tattoos of flames and a chrome trucker girl reading a book were inked on his forearm. He was in a good mood that afternoon because Joe had walked to the water bowl on his own that morning. We didn't have to call Dr. Dan after all.

We rode through Springfield's historic district, passed numerous antebellum homes with columns and porticos. We stopped at the red light near the courthouse. An antique store, a dance studio, a Christian bookstore, a Hispanic church, an organic market, and a tack shop surrounded the square. Springfield, Tennessee, has a population of almost seventeen thousand, the number of people it takes to fill the Nashville hockey arena. Its most recent claim to fame? A winner on a reality show called *America's Next Top Model* owned one of the nicer eating establishments.

The town's historic district represented a charming picture of the rural South; however, the second we crossed Memorial Boulevard the neighborhood changed.

Sycamore Street was tucked behind the Robertson County Jail, a bail-bonds office, a pawnshop, and a fast-food restaurant. The street measured maybe half a mile, all uphill. Sidewalks disappeared. Rows of cramped houses lined each side. Trash and weeds cluttered yards. The smell changed from fresh-cut grass and cedar mulch to chemicals spewing from the factories on Industrial Drive.

Bernice stood on the porch of a beat-down clapboard house. She was smoking a cigarette and wearing the same clothes she had on yesterday: sweatpants, flip-flops with socks, and the polka-dotted headband. For all the evidence of a tough physical life, Bernice exuded a naïve tenderness that bordered on childlike. I would later learn she quit school when she was twelve and didn't know how to read or write above a sixth-grade level. Her husband, Tray, was losing his sight and his foot from diabetes, and the hospital docked their social-security checks. I would learn the Lees were part of whatever class exists below blue collar.

When we met Bernice, Mason and I had only been fostering dogs for a year, but we already noticed a link between animal overpopulation and poor communities. Sycamore Street wasn't our first (nor would it be our last) encounter with impoverished neighborhoods in Robertson County. In fact, during our very first week of volunteering, Mason and I had rescued two mutts from a rural trailer park. The animals had lived in the front yard of a singlewide trailer that looked as though a tornado had picked it up and scattered its contents. Empty cigarette cartons, dirty diapers, buckets, plastic children's toys, an old camper shell, a waterlogged mattress, PVC piping, and Big K soda bottles were sprawled across the property. We eventually found out the family—a teenage mother, her boyfriend, and their three toddlers—split as soon as they received their eviction notice. If they couldn't fit something in their truck, they had ditched it, including their dogs.

I could tell Bernice was excited we were there, as though she didn't really believe we'd show up. She gave us a brief description of Night: all black with a white blaze down her neck. Bernice explained that she had shown up about four months prior; twice, she said. She'd never gotten closer to her than a few feet. I listened with forced patience, but I was only hearing half of her words because I was thinking about puppies; about roly-poly, pink-bellied puppies.

Finally, Bernice said, "I ain't seen Night since this morning, but I'll show you her babies."

Mason and I followed Bernice through a backyard where nobody had bothered planting grass. The smell of dirty cat litter clung to the humidity. An old condom, discarded needles, cigarette butts, and empty food wrappers peppered the ground. Sycamore Street wasn't only poor, but it was dirty. Mason looked as though the gritty neighborhood didn't faze him. He wore cargo shorts, a Beastie Boys T-shirt, and a Nashville Predators baseball cap pulled low. He would have worn the same outfit if we were in Manhattan. My husband looked comfortable anywhere he went. He exuded a self-possession that can only be described as that elusive trait known as *cool*.

Mason politely replied to Bernice's questions with, "Yes, ma'am" or "No, ma'am," and I recognized her surprise. Born in Kentucky, a southern gentleman was mixed in with all his coolness, and this quality always caught people off guard. With his tattoos and piercings, Mason doesn't look like the kind of person who pays attention to manners, but he does, and they are impeccable. It was one of the first things I'd noticed about him when I met him. The second thing I'd noticed was his voice. It's a deep baritone that sounds strong and dependable, as though the person who owns it is as solid as concrete, like that person won't crack under any emotional weight. Mason's analytical mind is a feature that took me longer to recognize, but I appreciate it as much as his manners and voice. In Bernice's yard, I knew that while I was obsessing over puppies, Mason was processing her property down to the holes in the chicken wire fence. He never graduated from college, but he had the mind of an engineer.

Bernice stopped outside a garden shed slumped against a patch of saplings. A bigger, sturdier barn stood thirty feet across from it. Both were boarded shut. Night had made her den inside an igloo-shaped bramble patch growing against the smaller shed. Its seclusion made it the ideal spot for hiding. Old oak and sycamore trees shaded it. Sunlight sliced through the foliage in shards that disoriented me, as though I was standing under a disco ball. It took a moment to adjust my eyesight, and in that second, something skirted past us. At first, I didn't know what it was. It could have been a cat darting under a branch or a child running across an adjoining yard. All I saw was a moving shadow. Finally, the outline of a dog's cockeyed ears materialized.

"That there's *Night*," Bernice said.

She said her name like she was awestruck. Her tone reminded me of the way I talked about rock stars as a teenager. I realized she not only cared about Night, but she idolized her. How could a dog she'd never touched inspire such awe?

I don't know how a canine measures distance, but when Night judged herself far enough away, she stilled. She wasn't a well-proportioned dog, but squat with a face too small for her body. Her dainty legs belonged on an animal twenty pounds lighter. Like Bernice had described, a white blaze streaked her chest, but otherwise she was all black. Her swollen teats hung several inches below her belly. They swished back and forth when she moved and made her appear clunky. With all that extra weight, she shouldn't have been able to run as fast as she did.

Night watched us with the timid, frightened stare of a rabbit or bird. She didn't have to say she didn't trust us. Her erect ears, lifted paw, and rigid tail screamed it. Trust doesn't rank on any list of essential human needs, yet living without it is a lonely existence. I know because I had grown up in a poor, mean town called Shickshinny, Pennsylvania, a place where a person's toughness was their credibility. In Shickshinny, the strongest ruled, and my home life had mirrored that culture. My father was an alcoholic whose mood shifted from exuberant to violent within seconds. One second he'd be eating stovetop popcorn on the couch, and the next he was ripping chimes off the wall or upending an armchair or dragging my mother by her hair across the foyer. Wariness had been a survival skill in my home.

As I stared at that filthy, nursing mutt, the distrustful little girl I'll always carry inside me woke up, the little girl who knew exactly how it felt to be afraid and unloved. It was the first time I laid eyes on Night; but in that instant, I felt as though I'd known her my whole life. Looking back, I realize it's also the moment when my promise to a stranger became a personal oath. I *would* catch Night. After seconds of scrutinizing us, Night disappeared behind a neighbor's house.

A few minutes later, I held a one-week-old puppy against my chest and, astonishingly, she didn't absorb every particle of my concentration. Sure, I sucked in a few hits of her warm breath, slid my pinkie across her closed eyelids, and cooed when she suckled my thumb; but the whole time I was looking for Night.

3

STRAWBERRIES

Joe Poop's bark wasn't angry, but it let me know he needed help. I worked in my office, a room away, but his call cut through my concentration, as though an alarm sounded next to my ear. He had earned the nickname "Poop" as a puppy because on two different occasions he pooped on a friend's pillow. Both times he had crawled onto Kevin Brown's bed, pranced across the comforter, squatted on his feather pillow, and dropped a whole pile of evidence.

I stopped typing and waited for the second bark, the one that meant he was serious. When Joe needed me, I wanted to be there. It was early summer and already simmering in Tennessee. I'd left Joe next to the water bowl, resting his stomach on the kitchen's cool tile floor. He used the stone's surface as natural air-conditioning. He had always been resourceful.

Outside my office window, three of our younger dogs played in our fenced backyard. They ranged from forty to sixty pounds and wore coats colored copper, black, and blond. They chased each other full throttle around the yard's perimeter. Their paws streaked through grass, leaving trails through the dew. They thrust their noses forward, flattened ears, and straightened tails, all in an effort to decrease air resistance. Finally, they collided under an ancient oak tree, where their game of chase morphed into a wrestling match. Displaying acrobatic grace, they leapt and twisted around each other. They nipped each other's ruffs and flashed their teeth. Mason and I lived with eight dogs during that year, and six of them were family.

Joe barked again, his tone weary. I pushed my chair from my desk. Dessie, our beagle mutt, snoozed below my feet. She sighed because my moving disturbed her. She readjusted her rump, rolled onto her back, and spread all four paws in the air. Dessie was a professional sleeper and spent most of her day snoring near an air vent. I once read that when dogs lie on their back with their belly exposed it means they feel safe and content. If that statement held any truth, then Dessie was, by far, the happiest dog in the house. She might have been the happiest dog in all of Robertson County.

Miss Annie followed me to the kitchen, paws clicking against the hardwood floors. She followed me everywhere, a tiny shadow prancing behind me like some kind of canine Tinker Bell. She wore a harness instead of a collar, and her tags jingled with a soft familiar ringing. Annie went straight to Joe's tail and sniffed. I ached to understand what she learned with one whiff.

Joe Poop sat in the same place where I'd left him, squatting on the tile floor in his now normal frog squat. He couldn't stand for longer than a few minutes, and ended up plopping down, knees bent like peaks along each flank. If I looked straight at him, without getting too close, I saw remnants of the old Joe. He still wore a beard and bushy eyebrows, but the rest of his fur was gone. His coat had shed away in clumps that started out as perfect circles, as though he'd been burned with a tailpipe.

Dr. Dan said Joe could go on living as an invalid for a long time. Dr. Dan was a giant man, well over six feet tall. He wore overalls and looked like he should be wrangling livestock instead of handling cats and dogs. He had red hair, an easy laugh, and compassionate eyes. For years, he had been taking care of Joe, performing everything from yearly vaccinations to an emergency injection of vitamin K after Joe ate arsenic in our neighbor's barn. Dr. Dan diagnosed his autoimmune disease. And he would be the one who euthanized him when we made that call.

I had prepared myself for this part of Joe's life, researched how he'd lose control of his bladder, bowels, and mobility, and how his energy would wither. I read literature about grief, burying versus cremation, and meditated over the profound loss of never seeing him again. But nothing prepared me for watching Joe's eyes fill with shame when he peed on his dog bed, woke up in his own feces, or nudged his chicken and rice away. A few years ago, I had met a grizzled Vietnam vet at an Independence Day parade. He was a man with overlarge ears, sideburns, and weathered hands, someone who'd survived war and all its atrocities. He claimed the pain of watching his German shepherd die made him never want another dog. I heard that sentiment voiced time and time again, but I was learning about the magnitude of it for the first time.

My bedtime ritual now included curling up next to Joe on the floor for a few minutes every night. I memorized the scruffy texture of his fur and wisdom in his eyes. I buried my nose in his black, callused pads. They smelled like the forest after a drenching rain. The scent reminded me of the first time I had stepped into the Jedediah Smith Redwoods State Park in Northern California. I've never been a spiritual person, but walking among those ancient trees, I had felt a profound sense of belonging to something bigger than myself. I got the same feeling smelling Joe's paws.

We had planned every step of euthanizing him, down to the New York strip we'd grill for his final dinner. And we asked ourselves the same questions each time he refused his food or wet his dog bed: *Was he suffering? Did he know how much we loved him?* And the most important question of all, *Were we keeping him alive for us or for him?* I experienced daily pangs of guilt for delaying what seemed inevitable, but the thought of watching that needle slide into Joe's vein was incomprehensible.

I looked into his cocoa-brown eyes.

"Do you need to go out, Poop?"

Guessing what Joe needed, what any of our dogs needed, was a constant challenge, a patient game of reading body language and accepting failure. Joe and I had gotten particularly good at this game of guessing.

Sometimes, Joe wanted to sit on the porch, so I pulled his pillow into the sunshine. Other times, he acted hungry, but that was increasingly rare. I had learned how the size of his pupils or the position of his ears, tail, and snout signaled whole worlds of meaning. I knew how to interpret Joe's basic needs. But when it came to the big stuff, like whether to make the call or not, all I heard was silence.

We stared at each other for a few moments of wordless communication, one blue human eye assessing one brown canine eye. Dogs can detect microscopic body movements, meaning Joe was better equipped at this game than I was. He glanced at the doggie door, back at me, then back at the doggie door. He wanted to go to the backyard. Joe recognized my awareness with a tail thump. I hadn't consciously moved a muscle, but some gesture, eyes widening or eyebrows lifting, communicated my understanding.

I scooped him off the floor. I picked up Joe several times each day and his lightness always startled me. He had been sixty pounds a year previously, but now he weighed forty-five. I carried him out the basement door and set him down in the grass. Joe wobbled, shuffled a few steps, and plopped down. His view included a wall of lush summer foliage and three young dogs playing.

"You okay out here, Joe?" I asked.

He lifted his face to the sun.

* * *

Writing a blog about fostering dogs meant I spent more time at my computer than I liked to admit. That day was no different. I got lost in my work and thirty minutes later realized Joe Poop was still outside. My office window looked over the yard, but blind spots blocked each side. Joe wasn't in my line of sight. I skirted down the hallway, through the kitchen and basement, and swung open the back door. I expected to find him frog squatting right outside, but he wasn't. Instead, he stood—or rather, teetered—in our garden, plucking strawberries off their stems.

I hadn't planted any vegetables or fruits that year. I hadn't tilled the soil or pulled any weeds, but the strawberries returned anyway. Joe's arthritis-riddled legs couldn't hold his weight for long, so he sank to the ground but continued grazing. A patch of wildflowers grew behind him and their petals dripped yellow, pink, blue, and purple. Cotton strands from the cottonwood trees caught on leaves and quivered in the breeze.

Joe looked regal in the center of it all, as though he ordered the day. A honeybee zoomed close to his maw, zigzagged away, returned. He snapped at it. The bee skirted away toward a sunflower. Creatures still listened to him, even now, even when he could barely walk on his own. Joe had always been the leader, the one who taught the younger mutts house rules, reprimanded unruly behavior with his signature no-nonsense growl. Who would lead when he was gone?

But he wasn't gone. He sat thirty yards away acting as though nothing else mattered besides those strawberries. I imagined the berry's tangy juice washing down my throat, the urge to eat another one as soon as the first disappeared. I smelled the fruit's strong acidic odor, felt its tiny seeds crunching between my teeth.

Before I could stop myself, I called out "Joe Poop." His tail swayed back and forth, back and forth. I said it again, "Joe Poop," quieter but firmer, etching it into the air, as though saying it out loud confirmed his existence. I felt as though every day of doubt and guilt had all been leading to this one, the one where he sat in the sunshine eating strawberries. His message was clear. Joe wasn't ready to die. Not today. We still had today.

4

My Tattoo

The tattoo on my right shoulder reads *m3jd*. The characters, all lower-case and all black, are the initials of my first pack. A middle-aged man with stringy hair and a leather vest inked it twelve years before I met Night. It hurt. It hurt like hell. The tattoo's design isn't creative or intricate, but a carbon copy I'd chosen from wall art displayed like posters at a Wal-Mart or Spencer's. A heart encloses the letters. A daisy dots the bottom. Lone Wolf wasn't a high-end shop, but it didn't need to be, not for what I wanted.

I've never worn a wedding ring. When someone asks me why I don't, I point to the tattoo and say those letters are the only reminder I need. I don't offer any more explanation because I can't articulate what that faded, cheap tattoo represents without sounding sentimental. How can I explain that Mason and those three dogs came into my life at a time when I didn't have a home or a family? How can I explain that, in our house, dogs hold as much value as humans? How could I ever make someone understand those dogs saved my life?

* * *

m2

After college, I lived in Virginia with Ben Cooper. We'd been dating for three years, living together for the last one. Ben playfully knocked, using our special rhythm on the door of our basement apartment. I already knew he planned on popping the question, but Ben wanted his proposal to be an event, the kind requiring pictures. These moments were important to him. I wanted special occasions to feel exceptional, but they didn't. They felt uncomfortable and staged. They reminded me of all the terrible moments—weddings, graduations, and holidays—I had spent with my father, moments when we were forced together because of tradition not love.

I lit a lavender candle, played Van Morrison, swept dust balls from the faux-wood laminate floors. Everything *looked* perfect, but that's not how I felt. I told myself that it didn't matter that Ben and I had spent the last two years putting each other down. It didn't matter that on most weekends we got drunk, then had spectacularly ugly fights. All that mattered was Ben wanted me. He knocked again, impatiently this time.

I swung the door open, and my life did change, but not because of Ben. He held a puppy who couldn't have weighed a pound. She was scared, cold, or maybe both, shivering so hard she looked as though she might crumble from the inside out. Her eyelashes were shiny, extraordinarily long, trembling along with the rest of her. I don't remember saying *yes* to Ben or the flash from the pictures. I don't even remember finding the diamond ring he tied around the Yorkshire terrier's neck. But I do remember the protective feeling that engulfed me the moment I saw her.

For hours afterward, I lay on our sectional sofa with Miss Annie. Ben had been on the phone since I'd said yes, calling his folks, confirming he had pictures, and already talking dates and places for the wedding. Miss Annie slept a few inches from my head. Her nose created the shape of an anchor, a shank with two arms grounding her to me. She didn't look real. Ever so gently, afraid my touch might make her disappear, I wiped my fingertip along each nostril, tracing the anchor's creases. When she didn't flinch, I brushed back satiny wisps of black and brown hair floating around her eyes. Carefully, she licked my finger. Then she licked it again. She had nobody else but me. Being without a family was a terrifying feeling. It must have been even more disconcerting for a dog who didn't speak our language. Miss Annie needed me as much as I needed her.

Over the next few weeks, her name morphed into a conglomeration of friends' suggestions until it became bigger than she was, a name so long it seemed royal: Miss Annie Daisy Banana Fanny. I was so in love with Miss Annie that I used her prefix to square out my own initial and scribbled $m2$ whenever I doodled on scraps of paper. I even painted it across the apartment's wall in purple spirals that stretched from floor to ceiling. A year later, I broke off the engagement and hawked Ben's ring, and $m2$ moved to Nashville.

* * *

$m3$

Mason's cell phone vibrated, stopped for a few seconds, then vibrated again. It was September 11, 2001. The pastel shades of a desert morning glowed outside the eleventh-floor window of the Flamingo Las Vegas Hotel and Casino. The light's hue washed out the neon fluorescents decorating the hotel's façade. The white linen curtains shimmied, propelled by air-conditioning blowing at a comfortable seventy degrees. The breeze caught the scent of my bouquet, daisies in an empty wine bottle, and circulated it throughout the hotel room. Mason and I had married in the hotel chapel the night before. Miss Annie had been my maid of honor and our only witness.

I edged toward consciousness in the same position I'd fallen asleep in a few hours before, spooning Mason's body, his curves fitting into my spaces like pieces of a broken whole. We were scheduled to fly to Pennsylvania for work that afternoon, but we still had another blissful hour or two before we needed to move. His skin smelled like cigarette smoke, perfumed sheets, hotel shampoo. We slept cocooned together in a California king mattress. The pristine white sheets stretched around us, but Mason, Miss Annie, and I cuddled in the center. The night before I'd drawn *m3* on the mirrors over the bed with lipstick.

Mason's phone rang for the third time in less than five minutes. I pressed my lips to his tattoo, the zodiac sign for a scorpion sketched between his shoulder blades. Miss Annie slept near Mason's chest, felt me stirring, licked my wrist. She didn't want to get up, either. Dogs weren't allowed at the Flamingo, but we'd put Annie in a backpack and carried her up in the elevator without anyone knowing. Over the past two years, I'd snuck Annie into stores, restaurants, parties, office buildings, a library, classrooms, and a television studio. I took Miss Annie everywhere, and if that meant doing it illegally, then I broke the law.

Mason and I had met in New Jersey at a racetrack during the last month of my rocky engagement to Ben. I worked as assistant director for the National Hot Rod Association's television package. Mason was an audio technician who set up microphones along a quarter-mile racetrack. He also worked on his father's super gas hot rod and talked about hauling it from California to Kentucky in that deep voice of his, a deepness that struck me as extraordinarily worldly and *cool*. I've always been a sucker for the cool guy.

His phone rang for the fourth time. Nobody called that much unless something was wrong. Minutes later, we gaped at black smoke funneling from the Twin Towers of the World Trade Center in New York City. We watched the aftermath of the attacks for hours, but we didn't understand how fundamentally our culture would change. We didn't understand how lucky we had been before 9/11.

Five days later, we flew home and discovered exactly how much it had changed. Being at McCarran International Airport felt more like being at an army base in a war zone. Officers were stationed at every entrance. They wore assault rifles strapped across their chest and all black or camouflage uniforms. Lines for check-in and security snaked through the dusky neon-lit hallways, yet the airport was absurdly quiet. At the gates, random people were pulled out of boarding lines and patted down or taken to small rooms with shut doors. Our fellow passengers moved with lowered eyes or looks of shock and fear. Too many were overly polite.

"It means something to me that we got married before all this," Mason said. "It means we're old school. And we'll always be old school."

I thought about the way Mason had asked me to marry him. We had been parked at the event warehouse for *Hot Rod* magazine in Memphis. He had dropped the car keys and couldn't find them. I must have said something sarcastic or funny because he busted out laughing, then spontaneously popped the question. It was just as simple as if he'd asked me where I kept a spare set of keys. He didn't have a camera or a ring. It meant he had cared as little for tradition as I did.

"We *are* old school, baby," I answered.

* * *

m3j

It was a picture-perfect afternoon for Nashville's 2005 Dog Day Festival. Sunshine covered Centennial Park, spread over the flowers at the Sunken Garden, the surface of Lake Watauga, the stairs of the Parthenon. The Parthenon was a life-size replica of the Athenian original, built for the World's Fair in 1897. Locals say it represents Nashville, which is nicknamed the Athens of the South. We'd moved thirty miles northwest of town to Robertson County a few years before, but that afternoon we drove downtown because of the annual dog festival. We went every year.

I attached Joe's number 25, written on red construction paper with black sharpie, onto his collar using a safety pin. I'd scribbled *m3j* on the back for good luck. I rubbed his head, telling him that win, lose, or draw, we loved him. Joe smiled, tongue hanging out, tail swaying back and forth. The hair around his ears was feathery, pointing in all directions. His ears perked up, except for the very ends, which flipped over like an envelope's flap. His beard was long, clumped with dirt, as though he'd been digging in the yard. I looked at Mason with that *Aren't you bathing your dog?* look.

"I had no idea he'd be entering a kissing contest today," he said.

Neither had I. It'd been a spur-of-the-moment decision.

Another one of those spur-of-the-moment decisions was adopting Joe. Mason and I had met him at a Nashville shelter called Love at First Sight! in 2001. He wasn't the cutest puppy in the shelter. He wore wiry white-and-black fur that sprung around his snout in awkward lengths; he had gangly legs and overlarge paws. As he aged, he grew a beard that reached his chest and made him look like a sage of yore. Mason said he was drawn to Joe because of the way he sat in his crate with all his weight resting on his rear. His front paws were hanging on the bars of his cage, as though Joe had been asking him to unlatch the door.

I printed JOE POOP on the entry sheet and hoped his funny surname might give us an edge. We didn't think he had a shot in hell of winning honorable mention, let alone the blue ribbon. The competition was stiff. Pretty women in flowing skirts carried pocket dogs that flicked their tiny pink tongues over their human's noses with dainty elegance. Great Danes and mastiffs, with names like Czar and Goliath, strutted next to kids and kissed entire faces with one swipe of their massive tongues.

Joe was as average as a mutt could be, but he had a special knack for kissing. He knew precisely how to lick, not too much or too slimy, but patiently. On that afternoon he acted like a seasoned pro, kissing with gentle, loving expertise. When the judge, the weatherman Justin Bruce from WKRN, called "Joe Poop" as the winner, Mason and I were stunned for a full second before we went nuts. We kicked the air like soccer parents after their kid had scored the winning goal. Poop just sat there, watching our unbridled joy, wearing a smile that said he never doubted his success.

* * *

m3jd

I drove slowly along our country roads. My eyes swept across landscapes that contained nothing but fields and forest. Occasionally, a truck pulled up behind me. I'd flick on my blinker and slow even more until they passed. Shoulders were nonexistent on these narrow roads. Occasionally, I stuck my head out the window and hollered Dessie's name, but the only answer was the wind rushing past my ears. Mason and I had moved to Cedar Hill five years earlier because we wanted privacy, but for the past week I cursed our decision. All of that empty space made finding Dessie that much harder. She wore a collar with tags and a microchip, but if nobody saw her, what good were they?

Dessie, our beagle mutt, had been missing for ten days, ten days that felt like forever. Mason and I had hung up posters at every four-way stop within a twenty-mile radius; we'd contacted shelters and put ads in the local papers. We'd driven our country roads from dawn to dark, but so far our efforts had yielded nothing but failure. Even so, we never talked about giving up. We couldn't, because our family felt fragmented every moment of those interminable two hundred hours. Dessie was missing, and nothing but finding her would make us whole again.

Miss Annie was napping on the front seat. Joe rested his snout out the back window. They knew something was wrong. They had known something was wrong for the past week. Their stoic demeanors gave it away. I felt the impossible but familiar urge of wanting to talk to a dog. I wanted to ask, Did they smell her? Did they hear her? Was I going in the right direction? *Was she still alive?*

Mason and I had been out of town for work when we learned she ran away. Our house sitter was walking Dessie off-leash in the woods behind our house when someone started firing a gun. Dessie bolted as soon as she heard the first shot. They had probably been target shooting because our sitter said the shots came in rapid succession. Dessie had had severe anxiety about loud noises since she was puppy. That wasn't the first time Dessie had run. Once, I'd opened the door of our Nashville apartment at the exact moment when someone set off a firecracker. The second time Mason and I had been at the grocery store when a thunderstorm cracked open the sky, and Dessie had wiggled through the fence. Each time, she'd returned after a day. This time she hadn't.

During the few hours I wasn't searching, I brushed Joe's fur. It was the only thing that calmed me. I worked through his coat from tail to snout with a fine-tooth comb. He liked when I brushed his stomach the most and kicked his rear leg in appreciation. I stored the loose hair in a plastic planter. One windy morning during those ten days, I released it all and watched the small tornadoes of hair disappear into the wilderness. I willed the swirling fur to find Dessie, to tell her we loved her, to tell her to come *home*.

I had met Dessie when I made the mistake of volunteering to play with puppies at Love at First Sight!, the same shelter where we adopted Joe. The shelter said the dogs needed interaction with people to help with their socialization. It was the perfect gig. I could do something worthwhile and get a few doses of puppy breath all at once. I diligently performed my duties for a full thirty minutes before I saw Dessie.

She caught my attention because she watched me so intently through the bars of her cage. Although she couldn't say a word, I heard her voice as clearly as if she'd whispered in my ear. She wanted me to take her home. When I pulled her out of her crate, I realized I was going to do that very thing. She was five months old with fluffy blond hair and a nose that looked like hot chocolate on a cold rainy day. Everything about her had felt comfortable, *familiar*. As though she completed our little family. A few days after we had named her, I got my tattoo: *m3jd*.

Rain drops splatted against the windshield. The sky darkened to a cinder block gray. I turned on my headlights and felt a keen sense of dread. Daylight was fading fast. Joe's eyes shined bright in the rearview mirror. I felt as though he was trying to tell me what I didn't want to accept. When the drops turned into a drenching rain, I turned toward home.

Before dawn on the eleventh day, Joe's barking woke me. He was frantic, yelling as though something or someone was on our porch. For half a second, my hopes soared. Was it Dessie? But Joe had sounded the same alarm so many times over the past week. And every time, I had swung open the front door full of hope, and each time I was disappointed. I was too tired to be disappointed again. He quieted down after a minute, so I fell back asleep for another hour. When his howls started again, they sounded even more urgent and insistent than the first time. I crawled out of bed, shuffled down the hallway, and opened the front door, fully expecting to see an empty stoop. But it wasn't empty. It wasn't empty at all. Dessie was curled up in the middle of our *Wipe Your Paws* doormat.

For a few off-kilter seconds, I thought I was dreaming. I had willed this moment so many times that I had to convince myself it was real. Dessie tentatively wagged her tail, a low-riding wag, like she might be in trouble. She hobbled over the stoop and collapsed on a dog bed, as though she'd been dreaming about that spot for days.

Her ribs were visible. She had lost at least ten pounds, meaning 30 percent of her body weight. Briars matted the long strands of fur on her stomach and paws. Her back leg hung limp. I gently moved her rear paw and saw a six-inch bloody gash inside her thigh. It reached the bone. It must have taken her days to hobble home. My questions were overwhelming: *Where have you been? What happened to your leg? How many miles did you travel?* But her only answer was that tentative tail wag. I realized I would never know. I'd never know where she'd been or what she'd seen, and somehow, none of that mattered. All I felt was joy. Our family was whole again.

Dr. Dan guessed she'd been stuck in a trap. After a weekend at the vet's office, antibiotics, a medicinal bath, and a bright yellow cast on her rear leg, she came home and never ran away again.

* * *

My tattoo is faded. Sunshine has diluted the colors. Mason jokes that it's my sailor tattoo, slang for it looks worn and cheap. For me, it's irreplaceable. I've come to realize it represents a distinct before and after in my life. It represents the difference between loneliness versus family, judgment versus unconditional acceptance. Before Mason and those three dogs came into my life, I really believed there was something wrong with me, something that made me unlovable. I also believed the cliché "blood is thicker than water." Since my father never cared about me, I wasn't worth anybody's love. It took surviving some chaotic years, but I finally found a family—an unconventional one, but a family nonetheless. And I didn't share a drop of blood with any of them. So, I asked a stranger in a Nashville tattoo shop to ink my family's initials on my arm, and I'll never regret it.

5

The Farnival

I kicked off my dusty sneakers and peeled off my sweaty socks. I wanted to shower the funk off my body, but it would have to wait. I needed to type up as many details as possible about our day, so I could eventually post an accurate description of Night on the Farnival. I hadn't written about her on my blog yet, and unfortunately, I didn't have much to report. I'd probably spent a total of a minute in her presence, and that may have been stretching it. The blog's name came from an accidental mash-up of the words *farm* and *carnival* after too many glasses of wine. Mason and I had been playing word games with friends over a firepit when I blurted it out. For some reason, it had stuck.

Mason was outside, helping Joe go to the bathroom. I couldn't see them, but I imagined Mason standing on the front patio with his careless slouch, smoking a cigarette. He'd watch Joe wobble around the grass or rest in his signature frog squat. The cicadas, frogs, and crickets chanted their evening song. In the summertime, the chirping is so loud it envelops our house. When we first moved to Cedar Hill, I couldn't sleep because of it. Now, I can't sleep without it.

It had made perfect sense to start a blog when we were fostering dogs for Free Love because it combined two of my favorite things, animals and writing. But I also started it because I wanted to raise awareness for all the homeless animals in Robertson County. I got the idea of writing about my county's animal overpopulation problem after I'd taken an online creative writing class with people from all over the country. Our instructor, a man from Boston, Massachusetts, asked us to write a scene in the voice of someone we would never be and perform an action we never would. I wrote about a woman who dropped off a litter of kittens on a country road.

My instructor said the act of unloading kittens on the street lacked credibility. He asked, "Why would someone need to drop a litter on the roadside when they could take them to a shelter?" My instructor's lack of awareness shocked me. Didn't he know about the animal overpopulation problem down here? Didn't he understand that most shelters don't even take cats, and if they do, there's normally a waiting list or a fee? Then, I reminded myself that I didn't know about the problem until I'd moved here, either. A few years later, I started writing about it. My idealistic self believed (and still believes) that if more people knew about the problem, more would help.

Annie and Dessie assumed their positions seconds after I sat at my desk: the little one on her dog bed, the bigger one under my feet. In cars, our dogs fell asleep as soon as the speedometer hit sixty. The same principle applied when I typed, as though the tapping of my fingers on the keypad lulled them to sleep. Whenever I stopped writing, Annie's eyes opened while she waited for me to finish a thought or leave my chair. She'd follow me if I left the room and go back to sleep if I didn't. Annie and I knew each other's body movements so well we communicated whole conversations without sharing a word.

Mason and I had spent the afternoon on Sycamore Street. It was our second visit. Bernice had been waiting for us on the porch, smoking and drinking coffee, just as she had the other day. Night must have heard us chatting, because we didn't make it around the house before she rocketed from her den. Dogs are creatures of habit. They like structure, so Mason and I thought if we mapped her route, she'd be easier to catch. We lost sight of her after five minutes, and spent the next hour hiking on hot asphalt without catching a single glimpse of her.

Mason supplied 50 percent of the Farnival's content, taking ten thousand pictures in two years. He often created photo essays of the dogs splashing around in neon kiddie pools or playing in our backyard. We tried updating the blog twice a week. My favorite entries were observations about the dogs' earthy-smelling fur or descriptions of their silliest games, like chasing frogs, eating cicadas, cleaning ears, or licking toes. The hardest posts were a series entitled "Euthanizing Joe."

I couldn't have completed a single sentence of that series if it hadn't been for the anonymous readers visiting our site every day. In some vast invisible cloud, I had formed relationships with complete strangers. Since I often posted silly stories or updates about our foster dogs, I felt I owed them the same treatment when it came to the tough stuff. In "Euthanizing Joe," I confronted why we were considering the decision to euthanize him. I described an incident when we were weighing that tremendous option, and Floyd, the only other male in our pack, lifted his leg and peed on Joe's dog bed, as though he was letting us know it was time for him to go. But I also wrote about the good stuff, like when Joe won the title of "Best Kisser in Nashville." The responses came from as far away as Seattle and as close as Springfield. People wrote stories about their own dogs or sent encouragement, letting me know I wasn't alone.

I finished typing up my notes on Night, took a shower, then crawled into bed. Miss Annie's tags jingled softly as she picked up the quilt with her nose. She repeated the motion until she raised it enough, then burrowed underneath the sheets and settled against my hip. She slept under the covers all night long. I heard Mason shut off the television and lock the front door. He dragged Joe's dog bed, with him on it, into the bedroom. When I woke up, Mason would be spooning me, and I would be spooning Annie. Joe would be watching us from the floor.

I posted three essays about euthanizing Joe, but I never wrote about our religious beliefs. Mason and I were atheists. Mason had been raised as a Southern Baptist; my family had irregularly attended a Methodist church. We talked about the afterlife early in our relationship and realized we shared Einstein's conviction when he said, "Energy cannot be created or destroyed, it can only be changed from one form to another." It's not that we don't *want* to believe in God, it's that we *can't* believe in him. Being an atheist isn't an easy road because it means acknowledging that when we die, our consciousness goes, too. It means there's no such thing as an afterlife. When Joe died, it meant forever, and when we died, it meant the same thing. I kept that part to myself because I wasn't brave enough to confront the permanence of goodbye.

6

Floyd and Sara

We passed Floyd and Sara, our youngest pack members, on an isolated country road in 2009, five years before we met Night. We were on our way home from an afternoon walk. Dessie and Joe stood on the folded-down backseat of my husband's 1992 Honda Accord station wagon and stuck their snouts out the windows. Annie napped on Mason's lap. He said that she picked that spot so she could keep her eye on me. In the rearview mirror, I watched Dessie's ears flutter like banners. She occasionally licked her nose, and her tongue flapped along with her ears. She didn't shy from the rushing wind but squinted and thrust her muzzle forward, as though she wanted to go faster. Her expression reminded me of riding on a speedboat over a calm lake, rushing through the atmosphere at speeds unachievable without an engine's power.

Ancient walnut, mulberry, sassafras, and sycamore trees edged both sides of Flewellyn Road. Their branches draped over the winding asphalt in canopies the highway department rarely trimmed. A rotten branch occasionally fell and blocked the roadway until someone with a pick-up truck hauled it away for firewood. That afternoon, the sunshine lit the autumn leaves in vibrant gold, red, and amber. Some drizzled onto the road, as though they had nothing but time. Others whirled in frenzied circles. It was a perfect fall day: sunny, temperate, and colorful—too pretty to see two starving dogs ditched on the roadside. But that's exactly what we saw.

Mason loved driving on Flewellyn because it curved like a slinky and tested his driving skills more than setting the cruise control on the highway. On the curviest section, he slowed considerably because of the snaking pavement, but also because of the wildlife. Squirrels, deer, turkeys, raccoons, groundhogs, and even an occasional cow crossed the road. When we passed two six-month-old puppies, we were moving so slowly that I had a long time to absorb their pathetic silhouettes. They were crouched by a farmer's gated access road. The copper dog caught my attention first because of his unusual red-orange fur, as burnished as a cedar tree's roots. He outweighed his sister by a few pounds. He sat hunched, not looking anxious but defeated, as though he'd given up. Then I saw the tinier pitch-black puppy, slumped against her brother, as though she didn't have the strength to sit up on her own. I didn't know how many days they'd been living on the street, but they weren't going to last much longer.

The road's seclusion made it an ideal spot for dumping dogs, which we knew all about because we saw at least one animal each year. The first year, we found a collarless mutt with long, matted fur, whom we vetted then put an ad in a Nashville paper. The next year, we picked up a beagle mix covered in engorged ticks. He had sat at the same spot as those puppies for a week. Finally, unable to resist those sad eyes, we took him home and paid for his basic vet bills and neutering. We rehomed him to a boy named Frank and his grandfather. They answered an adoption ad we posted in the *Bargain Browser*. The previous year, Mason and I had dropped off food for a terrier cur at the road's only STOP sign. I'd started feeding the dog after I saw her eating carrion. At some point, the terrier had disappeared.

All of those dogs had worn the same confused expression, as though they'd been ditched in a foreign country without a dime or voice to ask for directions. Even though canines are animals, they exist in a strange purgatory, trapped between two cultures, living somewhere along the continuum of natural instinct and domestication. Dogs' behaviors can still be very wolflike. But after living with humans for thousands of years, canines are dependent on people for their most basic survival needs, particularly food and shelter. For all their ancestral instincts, surviving in the wild is often as difficult for them as it would be for me.

"Did you see?" Mason asked.

"Keep driving," I said.

It sounds harsh, even now, but the practicality of taking home two sick dogs at that time was nil. In forty-eight hours we were flying to Dallas, Texas, and working for five days. Those dogs were obviously sickly. They could spread worms, fleas, or worse to Joe, Annie, and Dessie. Any contagious disease meant the dogs needed to be isolated. If they weren't, a sad situation could turn into a dangerous one for our pack and an expensive one for our family. Mason and I weren't independently wealthy. We lived on a budget with categories for clothes and car insurance, every penny doled into separate but necessary envelopes.

"They were pups," he said.

"We're working in Texas on Friday."

"Lino—" he started, but I cut him off.

"Those dogs are going to need more than Lino," I answered.

Lino Chavez is our house sitter, and one of my best friends. I met him walking on the Springfield Greenway a decade before he started taking care of our pack. He's a middle-aged Mexican immigrant who teaches our dogs basic commands in Spanish, but that's the extent of his training abilities. He loves animals and would wreck his car before hitting a squirrel, but he isn't an expert. Those dogs needed experienced medical and emotional care.

"If we don't do something, who will?" Mason asked.

That was the crux of the problem. Animal overpopulation is an epidemic in the rural South. Agencies like Free Love were nonexistent in Robertson County in 2009. Of the nonprofits operating outside our county, many had waiting lists or restrictions on health and breed. I'd once taken a litter of stray kittens to a Davidson County nonprofit, but they refused them because the kittens weren't "healthy enough." A nonprofit wasn't going to accept two sickly puppies in need of obvious medical care, and animal control would euthanize them out of necessity. If we picked them up, they were our responsibility.

We drove home in an uncomfortable silence. Mason brooded and pulled the brim of his Predators hat over his hazel eyes. He was pissed off. It was a rare occurrence. So rare that Miss Annie sensed it, and twitched her nose between us, as though she smelled the tension. Thirty minutes after we got home, Mason marched inside my office. The smell of tobacco clung to his long-sleeved T-shirt.

"I'm going back to look for them," he said.

I felt the word *no* rise in the back of my throat. *Push the issue, Melissa. Explain the complications that taking in two sick dogs posed for everybody involved. Say no.* Even with all these perfectly legitimate concerns, the word never left my mouth. Mason rarely asked for anything, and on that occasion, he wasn't asking. I had to respect what he wanted or fight him about it. Was it worth a fight? My initial reaction to seeing those dogs had been practical, but their pathetic silhouette remained fixed in my mind. My resolve had been weakening the whole time Mason's strengthened. In the far reaches of my brain, I'd already started figuring out how we could isolate them and where to squeeze money out of next month's budget.

Mason returned two hours later cradling the copper dog we named Floyd. Floyd was about six months old and emaciated, fifteen pounds stretched over a skeleton that should have held thirty. Mange, a parasitic mite, had eaten wide swaths of fur off his body. Mason wore a headlamp strapped around his baseball cap. His cheeks were bright red above his scruff. The forecast predicted temperatures would drop below freezing for the next week.

"The black one?" I asked.

"I couldn't find her," Mason said. "It's too dark now."

We found Sara the next day. As before, we passed her on our way home from our afternoon walk. She slumped against the access gate and stared at us like she'd been waiting. Mason looked at me. I shrugged my shoulders, knowing even if I actively protested he'd stop the car anyway. His compassion for animals is one of the many reasons I love him. He flipped on his emergency blinkers and pulled onto the shoulder.

Floyd recouped his energy in a brief twenty-four hours. After a medicinal bath and a few good meals, he bounced around our basement like any other curious six-month-old puppy. The worst part of his recovery was his mange, which we treated with weekly baths, but it meant he had to be isolated.

Sara had a tougher time recovering. She stayed at the Robertson County Animal Clinic with IVs pumping antibiotics and fluids into her system while we worked in Dallas. She suffered from starvation and mange like her brother, but a predator had also attacked her. Dr. Dan said a black buzzard or coyote left gouges on her paws and stomach. She couldn't walk without screaming for weeks because her pelvis and tail were broken. Dr. Dan surmised a car hit her and dragged her a few feet.

We kept Sara crated in my office with a baby gate at the door to keep the other dogs away. I poured all my energy into nursing her back to health. Every achievement, from urinating outside her crate to walking a single step, felt like a victory. Her integration with our pack was the Super Bowl. For months after Floyd and Sara regained their health, we talked about finding them homes. A few people were interested, but we always found a reason for saying no.

7

The Magic 8

Foliage shielded the rear of Night's den. An overgrown field spread for fifty yards behind the greenery. The narrow opening between the shed and the igloo-shaped thicket was the most exposed area, but the trees provided ample shade. Night's den was protected on all sides from intruders, but the puppies were still vulnerable to environmental conditions. I occasionally caught the sweet scent of wild honeysuckle, but the smell seemed more like a tease than relief on Sycamore Street.

Mason and I had brought two tarps: one to drape over the top of Night's den, one to carpet the bottom. The forecast predicted rain, not a drizzle but severe thunderstorms. Bernice's yard sloped. Any runoff could flood the den's bottom and possibly drown the litter. We hoped the tarps would help keep them dry and safe. That June it poured so often I often felt like we lived in the Amazon rain forest. Even the farmers didn't drive their tractors in the fields because they couldn't risk getting stuck in the slurping Tennessee clay.

"I'm going to survey the grounds," Mason said.

"There's ticks all over that field," Bernice answered.

Mason walked off in his characteristic unconcerned stride. His pace didn't give away one iota of the unease he must have felt about what he might step on or find. A cigarette hung from his mouth. He took his last drag, then rolled it between his fingers until the cherry smoldered to the ground. He stuck the butt in his pocket. Later, he'd throw it out in a trash can, or I'd find it in the washer. He never littered.

"That Mason," Bernice said.

I heard a familiar tenderness in her tone. Most southern women of a certain age developed a crush on Mace. Bernice was a small woman, bony and maybe five feet tall. Leaning sideways, she fit easily into the den. She pulled out the pups one by one and held each in the air.

"Oh, look at this one here," she cooed.

The puppies' eyes were sealed shut, muzzles squashed in wrinkles. Their ears stuck out from each side of their head. The flaps were barely big enough for covering the canal and looked more like an afterthought than a necessity. One day their ears would grow into one of their most distinctive features, shaped for capturing sound waves and funneling them to the eardrum.

I nuzzled a white one with a black mask and inhaled her sweet-and-sour puppy breath. The potent fragrance was uniform in each one, caused by an enzyme in their stomach necessary for breaking down Night's milk. That strange smell, found only in a pre-weaned puppy, always caused a reaction in dog lovers. They either loved it or hated it. For me, it was exhilarating and made me feel like anything was possible, even catching Night.

I placed the puppies on a towel we spread over the crabgrass and dirt. Night had delivered a large litter, two males and six females. White, blond, brown, and black colored their coats. Most wore multiple combinations of the four, but no two mutts looked the same. They wiggled on their pudgy bellies, moving more like seals than dogs. Their squat, unsteady legs couldn't hold their weight, so they gripped the blanket and tugged themselves forward one inch at a time. They stopped whimpering when they found a littermate. Clustering in the blanket's center, they squirmed on top and under one another until it became impossible to distinguish one dog's fur from the other.

I scooped up a brave one who explored the blanket's edge. The puppy nudged my T-shirt, probably mistaking my warmth for her mother's. Her toothless gums gnawed and tugged at the cotton.

Bernice canoodled a fat blond one with a white blaze on her forehead. She said, "This one here's mean. Listen."

The puppy growled, a soft rumbling deep in her chest.

I watched Bernice smiling over that insignificant sound, so soft we were the only ones who heard it. She felt the same way I did. She was puppy-stupid, a state when a person loses all logical sense. As a child, I hadn't played with dolls; I collected stuffed animals that I arranged on my rocking chair. I named them after characters in my favorite Judy Blume or fantasy book. At night, when our windows were black and impenetrable, when my parents were screaming and beating on one another, I'd stare at Frodo, Fudge, and Lucy and wish them to life so hard they had to move. In Bernice's backyard, it was as though my childhood fantasy came true, as though the stuffed animals on my rocking chair were alive. The fattest puppy rolled off the pile. He was dreaming, suckling and kicking his paws.

"What's he dreaming about?" I asked.

"That fat one's a boy, ain't it? He's dreaming about titties. He'll be dreaming about titties for the rest of his life."

We laughed until our sides hurt. The dirty yard, Night's distrust, even euthanizing Joe—all of it faded into the background. In that moment, Bernice and I acted like schoolgirls brought together by eight dogs nobody cared about except for us. Those puppies were magical before they could even see. That's when I nicknamed them the Magic 8.

My magic moment busted when I noticed a flea on a white puppy. Then I was right back on Sycamore Street, squatting in a littered yard, playing with stray puppies. Once I saw one flea, I saw another, then another. If flea infestations aren't controlled, they can cause numerous illnesses. They can even kill puppies.

I felt a wave of hopelessness, knowing no matter what we did these dogs were vulnerable until we permanently moved them to a safe environment. I also knew that if we ignored the fleas, the infestation would only get worse. They didn't have anybody else but us; and right then, we didn't seem like nearly enough.

* * *

Mason kneeled over Nancy Padfield's shoulder and zoomed his lens on a puppy she held over a galvanized tub. He was taking pictures of the Magic 8 getting their first bath. Stationed on the opposite side, I gave the runt the same treatment. The largest and smallest were the only males. The smallest was half his brother's weight and pure black, a miniature replica of Night. I had Googled the safest way to kill fleas on young pups and discovered Dawn detergent was the answer. I knew Bernice wouldn't have the resources available for bathing the dogs, so I had immediately called my friend Nancy.

Nancy was fiftysomething, adventurous, and hilariously sarcastic. She lived with her husband and their two teenagers five minutes away from Bernice's house. The Padfields owned a *clean* brick home with a paved driveway and garage. They had a tub, a hose, towels, and detergent—all the resources we needed for bathing eight puppies.

Nancy's hands were manicured, with smooth skin and painted fingernails. Thirty minutes ago, I had been watching Bernice's nicotine-stained fingertips and callused palms holding those same puppies. Nancy and Bernice were probably around the same age, yet Nancy looked ten years younger. She acted a decade younger, too, and walked four miles every morning. Bernice probably didn't walk the sum of Sycamore Street. Living poor had aged Bernice.

We gently scooped water over the pups' bodies and scrubbed Dawn into their fur. Amber-brown insects squirreled out of the fur on their eyelids, ears, tails, and paws. They wiggled out of their muzzles' squashed folds and scurried across their roly-poly bellies. They inhabited every crevice available. Nancy and I probably plucked a thousand fleas that day.

I was drawn to the different shades of pink on all the body parts I inspected. The pads of the puppys' paws were coral, tongues rosy. Their stomachs wore the same flush as a child's toes. Some mewled, some squirmed. They all relied on their hardwired instincts because as soon as they felt water, they pumped their legs, as though trying to swim. For the first time since I drove onto Sycamore Street, I felt like I was doing something right. Joe wouldn't get better. Night didn't trust us. But I could keep those puppies clean.

"How's Joe?" Nancy said.

"Not good."

"Why can't they just walk off in the woods and die on their own?" she asked.

"That only happens in the movies," Mason answered.

Mason and Nancy had the same conversation whenever anyone we knew had to euthanize their animal. Nancy always asked the same question, and Mason offered the same response, as though if they said it enough it would come true. There was no good way to lose a dog we loved like Joe, but I daydreamed about a scene in that movie Nancy and Mason talked about. I pictured Joe sleeping on his favorite spot in the backyard, dirt flattened as hard as rock from years of his weight. In my dream, I wouldn't even know he passed until I checked on him. That's how I wanted Joe's life to end, like a movie scene, all neat and tidy with pictures to fill in the blanks and an ending wrapped up with credits and music. My fantasy was romantic and selfish, but I imagined it over and over during those last days.

We had been protecting Joe since Mason spotted him in that cage. We fed him, gave him daily vitamins, medicated him each month for fleas and heartworm, got him vaccinated each year, and ensured he had dental treatment. We cared for his stitches when he sliced his skin on barbed wire and rushed him to the hospital when his nose bled uncontrollably after his arsenic-eating incident. We trimmed his nails, brushed his wiry hair, picked briars from his beard, clipped flyaway fur around his eyes. Our role as his protectors set against euthanizing him presented a very cruel contrast.

Besides asking about Joe, Nancy peppered us with questions about Night. Later, I would learn that most people who heard about that dog wanted to know more. On a normal day, our blog received about two hundred hits; but when we introduced Night, it spiked to six hundred. *What does she look like? How old? Is she aggressive?* Nancy offered suggestions on catching her, like baiting her with a Wendy's cheeseburger or trapping her inside her den.

"What am I going to call Night on the Farnival?" I asked.

Nancy had lived in middle Tennessee for twenty years but still retained a faint New Jersey accent. She wore the silliest of smiles while she bathed the pups, and I realized those dogs had the same effect on her that they did on Bernice. Nancy and Bernice were so different, but those puppies ignited the same protective instincts in both of them. It was even more proof of the pups' magic, more proof that animals unite us. Nancy dropped a dab of Dawn in her hand and lathered a puppy's head.

"You should call her Dawn," she said.

I shrugged. Why not?

"Dawn it is," Mason said.

From that point forward, we called her Dawn everywhere except for Sycamore Street. I later tried introducing Nancy's suggestion to Bernice, and in an ironic twist Bernice took the name change so personally that I never brought it up again.

We'd taken the flea-infested pups to Nancy's house wrapped in a faded orange blanket. We returned them to Bernice's backyard swaddled in a woven basket with coordinating blue-and-yellow blankets. Mason ended up taking two hundred pictures that day. I posted three. My favorite one captured all eight in the basket. A blond puppy is the only one with her face outside the blankets. The rest are cuddled underneath it. On first glance, the blond puppy could be the cover girl for any number of feel-good cards or calendars. But if I stared long enough, I could make out a thin line of dirt marring the crease around her pink nostrils. We'd washed those puppies twice with detergent, but we still couldn't scrub Sycamore Street away.

* * *

Bernice's house was the third one from a dead end. A driver's only option was turning around in an abandoned lot or taking a sharp right onto Cheatham Street, where Sycamore Street ended. Bernice's front porch held two folding chairs, a plastic coffee table, and a bucket filled with fresh water for neighborhood dogs and cats. She'd also arranged blankets as bedding for these same animals. When we returned from Nancy's house, Joan Pryor was sitting in a chair and drinking coffee with Bernice on the porch. They looked like they'd been friends for years.

A key ingredient to catching Dawn had been getting support from Joan, Free Love's director. From a purely pragmatic level, Mason and I couldn't assume financial responsibility for nine more dogs if we planned on feeding the ones who already lived with us. Originally from North Carolina, Joan loved the theatre, wore kitten heels, and had a musical southern voice. She had started the nonprofit in 2012 after volunteering at Robertson County Animal Control and realizing how many dogs in our county needed help.

Free Love didn't have a facility. Joan ran her rescue through a network of foster families, who invited stray dogs into their houses and treated them like family until she found suitable homes. She also ran her nonprofit with a practical, no-nonsense attitude, which is the reason she was successful on such a small budget. She rejected more pleas to help with animals than she accepted. It wasn't an easy stance, but it was necessary. She knew her organization's limits and rigidly stuck to the bottom line. Joan couldn't rescue mass numbers of dogs, but she could save one at a time.

During that summer, for whatever reason, the universe aligned. Maybe Dawn and her litter arrived at a time when the nonprofit had a few extra dollars, or maybe Joan knew Mason and I needed a distraction from Joe. I'm not sure why it happened, but after a brief phone conversation Joan had volunteered Free Love's help without any argument. She'd been making arrangements ever since. She had asked the vet about caring for pre-weaned puppies and found a foster family who lived on a farm. If we caught Dawn, the family had offered their barn as a place for her to live until the pups were weaned. It was one of the many ideas we accepted and then later rejected, because Dawn outsmarted us all.

Joan said she had come over because she had an idea for catching Dawn. One of Joan's contacts at Springfield Animal Control recommended putting the pups in a crate to lure Dawn inside. Her contact said they regularly used live traps to catch strays. Free Love didn't own a live trap, one that sprung shut on its own, but we had an extra-large crate where we could move the pups. When Dawn went inside to feed her litter, Bernice could simply latch the door. It wasn't a well-coordinated attempt, and in retrospect, it was naïve. But at that time we were so new at catching feral dogs that it sounded like a plausible idea.

"How long since the puppies ate?" Joan asked.

"Two hours," I replied.

"We have three more before they need to eat again," Joan said.

We positioned the crate near Dawn's igloo-like thicket and blocked all sides except the entrance with a tarp. We bundled the puppies in a blanket, placed them near the back, then went home and waited.

Bernice called two and a half hours after we left. She said Dawn wasn't feeding her pups. She wouldn't go inside the crate. Dawn whined and paced outside of it, but she wouldn't even stick her head through the door. The puppies needed to eat soon. Bernice said it didn't matter anyway because she couldn't walk the length of her yard. She had pulled her sciatic nerve. Mason strapped on his headlamp, drove ten miles to town, and moved the litter back to their bramble patch. The next morning Bernice reported Dawn had spent a rainy night inside the thicket feeding the Magic 8.

8

THE SOPRANOS

I went through my third episode of clinical depression three months before I fostered my first dog for Free Love. During the worst of it, I spent twenty hours a day in bed, only I wasn't sleeping. I couldn't sleep because the enormous weight of nothingness crushed my rib cage until breathing was a chore. Blinds shaded my bedroom in the gray tones of a cloudy evening. If I inched up the blinds, I could see the multiple green hues of spring, but they'd been closed for months. It was winter inside our house, frigid and dark.

In my mind, my serotonin-deficient brain, I was convinced that cancer filled every part of my body, slowly gnawing my insides. I had greasy hair and terrible body odor; half an inch of shag grew on my legs and under my armpits. My house was filthy, too. Dog hair collected in tufts up and down the hallway, as though they were tumbleweeds blowing across an abandoned Texas town.

My self-worth had bottomed out in the negative digits five months after I left a fifteen-year career in television production. It was a time of drastic flux in my life. I went from a job that required traveling to twenty-four different cities each year to living in the southern countryside full time. These life changes coupled with a foolish decision to stop taking my daily dose of fluoxetine sent me spiraling into a clinical depression. I quit the antidepressant because it was allergy season. Antihistamines left me shaky, and the antidepressant made it worse. I rationalized that I hadn't relapsed in sixteen years, and it'd be safe to go without the fluoxetine for a few months. Wrong answer.

I lived with a constant sense of shame that spring. I went out in public as little as possible. It was hard enough witnessing Mason's disillusioned glances, let alone facing complete strangers' inevitable judgments. I only left my bed when I had to use the bathroom. When Mason was home, when he watched me shuffle from room to room, I saw his hazel eyes fill with disappointment, the kind of disappointment that comes with finding out that what you believe isn't real.

A few years ago, Mason and I had been walking along the Ohio River in Owensboro, Kentucky. We were in to town to visit his parents. From afar, I saw a lanky young man, maybe early twenties, fishing off a dock. A crystalline sky framed his silhouette while a breeze tousled his translucent fishing line. The scene filled me with a sense of nostalgia, an appreciation for nature mixed with a certainty of its impermanence.

As we passed the fisherman, he turned a bag of potato chips upside down, then casually tossed the aluminum wrapper in the river. It took a few stunned seconds to replace my original assessment of simplicity and nature with a man throwing trash into the river. But once the adjustment happened, all I had felt was disappointment. When I was depressed, Mason looked at me the same way, like I wasn't who he thought I was and that reckoning surprised him.

The only company I craved during that time was Miss Annie and Tony Soprano. Annie's six-pound weight was the only measurable part of my life. Miss Annie never left my side, not once. She curled into a ball against my hip, hair as soft as velvet. I'd run my pinky across her little wet nose, that anchor-shaped nose, as though some cosmic force interceded when dogs were designed. At the darkest times, the times when I didn't know if wanted to wake up ever again, when I planned my suicide down to the exact minute I'd swallow the pills, she kept me anchored to the here and now. There were even moments when I ruled out suicide simply because no one else could take care of Annie like me. She was so much a part of me that in some region of my mind, I believed if I died, she would, too. As though we only existed because of each other.

My feelings about Tony Soprano had more complicated roots. *The Sopranos* is an HBO crime drama that first aired from 1999 to 2007. During that spring, I played all six seasons of the show, one after another from dusk until dawn. Sometimes, I didn't even watch but just listened. As much as I needed Miss Annie's weight, I needed Tony's voice. A large part of my obsession stemmed from the fact that Tony also suffers from clinical depression. It runs in his fictional family as predictably as it runs through my real one.

In the first season, during the episode "Isabella," Tony confides to his psychiatrist, "Getting stabbed in the ribs is painful. This shit . . . I don't feel nothing, nothing. Dead. Empty. Everything I touch turns to shit. I'm not a husband to my wife, not a father to my kids, not a friend to my friends. I'm nothing." When I heard those words, it felt as though Tony Soprano held a megaphone to my brain. Like Annie, he eased my loneliness because he understood.

But his mental state wasn't the only reason I clung to him back then. I also needed Tony because my inner little girl needed a father. I wanted someone to protect me because I was scared and sick, and I wanted that person to be a mob boss. Tony is a cheating, murdering, lying, thieving narcissist, but he loves his daughter Meadow, unconditionally. In the last season of *The Sopranos*, a mobster from a rival family confronts Tony's daughter in a restaurant, and says she has cream on her lip. He caresses her cheek. Meadow tells her father about Coco's threatening behavior later over their kitchen table.

I watched the episode "The Second Coming" a hundred times. Each time, I couldn't tear my eyes off Tony's face as he processes Meadow's story. His rage is palpable. It's so powerful he can't sit still. He has to act, has to punish the man who violated his daughter. In the next scene, Tony storms through the restaurant, knocks Coco to the ground, then kicks his teeth out against the tile floor. His message is clear: nobody fucks with Meadow Soprano.

From my earliest memories, my father was the anti-Tony, the antagonist of my nightmares. I didn't run to him like Meadow ran to Tony; I ran away from him. I ran away so much that in middle school my friends sang Bon Jovi's "Runaway" whenever I passed them in the hallways. But even before he was violent with me—before he strangled, punched, or restrained me, before his strength rendered me submissive or sent me fleeing—he scared me. I can't remember a time when I wasn't afraid of my father.

When I was nine years old, our longhaired barn cat had a litter of kittens. My younger sister Mandy and I were each allowed one. I tied a pink ribbon around the kitten I named Taffy and a blue string around Mandy's Coco. The rest went to whoever answered the "Free Kittens" sign my father nailed on a tree near our mailbox. Both cats were orange and looked like their mother, but their personalities were vastly different. Taffy napped or cuddled twenty-two hours a day, while Coco ransacked the barn hunting for birds, mice, moths, and dust balls.

For months, I spent every afternoon sitting on a hay bale, reading *Tales of a Fourth Grade Nothing* and *Superfudge*, while Taffy purred on my chest and Coco played with my hair ribbons. Multicolored ribbons were strewn across the floor. They weren't thin or shiny, but hefty, made of a thick cotton-wool blend, as though they'd been knitted. I used the same kind for their collars.

One afternoon, my father was grabbing some garden tools out of the barn. The ribbons annoyed him, and he started shoving them in a garbage bag. Coco must have thought he came to play because he swatted my father's hand and sliced his skin deep enough to draw blood. My father was probably tipsy or already tanked because he picked up a hammer and whipped it at Coco, who screeched and scrammed for the rafters. In retrospect, I knew Coco was doomed as soon as I saw the look of rage that crossed my father's face.

That night, a shotgun blast pierced through the cool autumn Pennsylvania evening. The quiet afterward sounded as loud as the explosion. I raced downstairs, the silence pushing me faster. My mother sat at the kitchen table bent over her checkbook and a calculator. She acted as though nothing was wrong. The windows were black mirrors that reflected her perfectly coiffed curly hair. Gold bracelets glimmered from her wrists. She looked so normal, so calm, I questioned whether I had heard anything at all.

"Your father shot a skunk, that's all," she said.

Two days after the gunshot, I found Coco's collar. At first, the ribbon blended with the dead leaves. Dried blood colored it a similar bark brown. I reached for it, sure but unsure, wanting to know yet screaming against it. It was stiff and crusty, but there was no denying it had been Coco's blue ribbon.

In retrospect, my need to protect the defenseless started with finding Coco's collar. My focus on dogs wouldn't coalesce until years later, when I met one called Puff; but that was the moment when speaking for those who couldn't speak for themselves became important to me. Back then, some part of me blamed myself for Coco's death. If I had acted, if I had hidden Coco in my closet or taken him to a neighbor's shed, if I hadn't egged him on or left the ribbons scattered across the floor, maybe he would have lived. In a way, every time I save an animal, I'm giving back to that little girl inside me who will always blame herself for her father's mistakes. For me, my depression, rescuing animals, and my obsession with a mob boss are entwined with that bloody blue ribbon. It's where all three of them began.

I watched the final episode of *The Sopranos* the first time it aired, sitting on a king-size mattress in a hotel room in Englishtown, New Jersey. I didn't plan it that way, but it seems fitting that I watched the ending in Tony's state. Tony meets his family in a diner. "Don't Stop Believin'" by Journey plays on a jukebox. An ominous-looking gangster walks out of the bathroom. The implication is that he's a hit man sent to assassinate Tony. Then the screen cuts to black.

Like millions of people, I thought some catastrophe had occurred or the cable went out. I opened the hallway door, waited for fire alarms to start ringing. I called the front desk. The manager assured me that the hotel hadn't taken a power hit. The cable was fine. The next morning, I found out the series had intentionally ended with a black screen, an unknown, a question mark. In other words, I got to make up my own ending. So, in my version, Tony Soprano never dies.

After that last bout of depression, I returned to civilization as though hiking through snowdrifts—but I returned. I'd been ill for months, bedridden for two. The doctor said I'd been low for so long that the anti-depressant would need time to build up my serotonin level. Miss Annie stuck with me every step of the way, her tiny paws pitter-pattering behind me, her eyes a constant reminder that I wasn't alone. I wasn't unloved. Three months after my depression ended, I started fostering dogs for Free Love. I named all the homeless mutts after *Sopranos* characters.

9

FIGHT OR FLIGHT

Two of the fattest pups belted out piercing cries from Bernice's stoop. We picked the fattest because they were the healthiest. Their yelps cut through the cicadas chirping, children playing, a neighbor arguing with his wife. I smiled. We wanted them screaming. We'd been waiting thirty minutes to hear their screaming. If our second attempt at catching Dawn worked, their cries would lure her onto a stoop on the left side of the house. The landing was barely big enough to hold a grill, but its wrought iron fence, four steps, and narrow opening made it the perfect place to trap her. The second she walked onto the landing, Mason would slip out of his hiding spot and block the entryway with a baby gate. The hardest part would be coaxing her into that small space. We'd placed a Wendy's cheeseburger on the middle step, just in case the crying pups weren't enough motivation.

I signaled to Joan, who waited beside me at the edge of the front porch. Joan whispered into her cell phone, "The pups are crying."

"About time," Bernice said. She watched from inside her house, keeping tabs out the back window. We were on a three-way call.

"Copy that," Mason said. He hid in a cinder block nook on the right side of the home, so we had the whole perimeter covered. Mason didn't hunt, but he possessed a hunter's patience. I pictured him leaning against the house, smoking his cigarette, unfazed by how long it took Dawn to appear. I'm sure he was the epitome of coolness.

Unfortunately, I didn't possess Mason's patience. We'd been waiting for thirty minutes, but it felt like a hundred years. The temperature had reached ninety degrees, eighty percent humidity. Sweat trickled down every crack in my body. Gnats, mosquitoes, and flies zigzagged around my baseball cap and landed on my shins, arms, and ankles. Every second itched more than the last. So many flickering shadows caught my attention that I questioned whether or not Dawn was within hearing distance of her pups. I questioned our whole plan.

As though Mason had read my mind, he cautioned, "Patience."

Mason hadn't grown up with animals. In fact, even now his mother won't allow a dog to walk through her front door. But Mason never questioned why I treated animals with as much respect as humans. When we first met, he had often teased that I wore a neon sign reading, MUST LOVE DOGS, BUT MUST DOTE ON MISS ANNIE. He said he had known what he was getting into from the first time he saw the way Annie and I threw ourselves at each other after a weekend apart. He didn't complain when Annie slept under the sheets or when she licked the leftover salmon and broccoli straight off my plate. He didn't raise an eyebrow when she slept on the bathroom rug while I showered, took a bath, or used the toilet. He didn't roll his eyes when I made social plans around whether Annie could come or not. Mason simply adapted to our lifestyle as though he belonged, as though he'd always belonged.

"Dawn," Joan whispered.

Dawn appeared under a neighbor's carport, standing so still it seemed like she'd been there all along. She stood next to a crumbling birdbath with green water swamping inside. Her pitch-black color served as the perfect camouflage. I recalled a story a neighbor had once told me about his barn cat and her litter. A fox or coyote had killed all of them except for one black kitten. My neighbor said the little guy probably survived because the killer couldn't see him. Watching Dawn, I understood exactly what he meant.

Dawn could have used any shadow as protection, and there were thousands of them on Sycamore Street. I never noticed how many shadows existed until I searched for a black dog. Houses, telephone poles, mailboxes, parked cars, lampposts, bicycles, garbage bins, sheds, and shrubs, all of the things that comprised a neighborhood, disguised her. She could have stepped a foot in any direction and disappeared as suddenly as she emerged.

Dawn didn't make a lot of noise, either. She didn't wear dog tags or a collar, so no jingling announced her presence. Even with the weight of her teats, the brawniness of her rib cage, she walked with a sparrow's light step. Her eyes looked anxious, flitting here and there, as though she might dart away, as though she was temporary.

"She's here," Joan whispered into the phone.

"Copy that," Mason repeated.

The puppies' cries intensified in pitch and urgency, as though they sensed their mother. Dawn lifted her front paw and strained her ears forward. She wasn't a thin dog. Unlike most of the homeless dogs we met, she obviously ate well. She didn't need food. She needed a home.

In the dictionary, the word *stray* means "not in the right place or not having a home." When I was a child and then a teenager, I felt like I lived in the wrong place, like I was a stray. From my first memories, I recognized that I was fundamentally different from my family, physically and mentally. My parents are short and dark and sedentary. I'm tall and fair and athletic. I wanted to live anywhere except Shickshinny, whereas my parents belonged there. Whereas I pointed out everything wrong with my small town, my father fit in perfectly. He once told me that I was hard to love, and I believed him. I believed him long after I left home. I believed him until I met Miss Annie, until we became a family. Watching Dawn, I knew she didn't understand her feelings or reflect on their cause, at least not in the same way I did. But I know that she felt just as lonely as I had for all those years. She felt scared and unlovable, as though she *had* to hide. She had to hide because being close to people meant pain.

Dawn suddenly sprinted across the road and trotted to the stoop. She spent a few minutes investigating the grass, concrete, and gravel around the bottom of the stairs. She placed one paw on a step and sniffed some more. Several times, she tried stepping on it and shifted her weight forward, but she always backed down again. I saw Mason sneaking behind her at the same time it hit me she'd probably never gone up stairs. I wanted to warn him, but screaming would end any chance we had of catching her. I reached for Joan's phone.

"Wait, Mason, wait."

Radio silence.

Mason couldn't see her anxious behavior from his position. He didn't know she wasn't familiar with steps. We had witnessed this hesitancy before in foster dogs. Many had never lived inside a house, so they often acted jumpy around vacuums, brooms, ceiling fans, window fans, television sets, the clothes dryer, and dishwasher, even doors swinging open. They rarely understood how to ride in a car or walk on hardwood floors. Most didn't know that dog beds, squeaker toys, and rawhides even existed. More often than not, they didn't understand the concept of using stairs, either.

Dawn smelled or saw my husband, stopped, and whipped her head backward. The look on Mason's face registered his surprise. She should have been on the landing by then. For a solid ten seconds they stared at each other, as though they were sizing each other up. Joan and I stepped into the yard and blocked Dawn's road access. Twenty yards separated us. She was trapped.

Bernice stormed outside. The screen door slammed shut behind her, slapping the doorframe with a resounding crack. Dawn flinched at the sound, as though someone had exploded fireworks in her eardrum. Her nervous system switched into overdrive, and her survival instinct triggered her fight-or-flight mode. And she wasn't a fighter. Being pack animals, dogs calculate strength in numbers. In a split second, she probably weighed her odds and decided she had a better chance of slipping past Mason than the three of us. She launched forward. Mason leaped.

For a split second, my hopes soared, but they crashed right back down when Mason landed on Bernice's yard empty-handed. Dawn scooted past him, as agile as a running back for a professional football team. She disappeared into the empty field behind her den. Waves of goldenrod, horseweed, and ryegrass closed around her.

"I had my hand on her," Mason said. "I touched her."

Things changed between Mason and Dawn after that day. Dawn recognized Mason and disappeared the second he showed up on Sycamore Street. He couldn't get out of the car before she beelined it for the field. He had become a recognized threat, the proverbial "dog catcher." The opposite happened with Mason. Up until then, catching Dawn had been a diversion, something to keep his mind off Joe. But Mason's investment changed after that incident. He set his stubborn analytical mind on catching that stray, and he never let go, as though that near miss somehow ate at him, as though touching her bonded them. Even when I was on the verge of giving up, even when I *had* given up, Mason never stopped trying to catch Dawn.

10

FLEAS

The Magic 8 slept in a mound at the center of a faded beach towel decorated in sandcastles. Sunshine slid through the rusted trellis on Bernice's porch and washed their downy fur in a warm glow. The puppies had been in our lives for ten days. They were almost two weeks old. If I kept my eyes trained on the towel, didn't peep beyond the last sandcastle, I could pretend they were somewhere safe. Joan, Bernice, and I had just bathed them again with detergent. The tarps had kept their den dry during the thunderstorms, but the fleas returned with a vengeance.

"They have to be eight weeks old before we can put a pesticide on them," Joan said.

She was trying to convince Bernice we should move the Magic 8 to a safer environment, even if we didn't catch Dawn. We had no intention of breaking our promise to catch Dawn, but things had gotten more complicated. For one thing, Dawn was wilier than any of us had expected. We had finally realized that trapping her was going to take research and planning. For another, the puppies' safety was a huge concern. Before long, they'd start to wander, and we didn't have a lot of faith they'd survive in a weed patch behind Bernice's house.

The puppies' eyelids were opening, but their retinas weren't developed yet. A cloudy blue-black color that looked like cataracts filled their eyes.

I'd seen the milky eye in puppies before, but I'd never realized each eye opened at a different pace, even on the same dog. Half of them squinted. Their damp fur smelled like a mix of wet tree bark, cut grass, and mud. They bundled around each other, sticking their snouts, tails, and legs in any unoccupied space. A black pup stretched her pin-size claws into the air, repositioned her weight. Everyone else adjusted accordingly. They inhaled in waves, one swelling chest after another, and exhaled sweet-and-sour puppy breath. I'd bottle that smell if I could. The puppies were dialed into each other's movements in a way that could only have come from being mashed together in Dawn's womb for three months.

"Eight weeks. That's well over a month from now," Joan said.

Bernice answered with a story about a different stray called Gamma, who had been in a similar situation as Dawn. A neighbor had called Robertson County Animal Control about the longhaired mutt who delivered a litter under a porch. Animal Control took the pups and promised they'd come back for Gamma, but they never did. I'd heard similar tales before and understood both sides of the dilemma. Puppies are easy to adopt out, but grown dogs often occupy valuable space in overcrowded facilities for months, and our animal control offices rarely had room.

Bernice chain-smoked her long, skinny menthol cigarettes. She lit the next one off the butt of the last. Joan was rattling her. I wanted Joan to win, *really* wanted her to win, but I also felt sorry for Bernice. Over the past ten days, we'd spent so much time together that I'd started to care about her. She didn't have a driver's license, so I had given her a ride to the discount tobacco store, her mother-in-law's house, H. G. Hill for groceries, and Vanderbilt Hospital in Nashville. Bernice liked to talk, and she didn't hesitate to share personal details. In a matter of days, I learned she grew up with an abusive mother, had a thirty-pound cat named Pork, and had a sister with a pet squirrel. Bernice was a simple woman with a tough past, but she had an enormous heart.

I sat cross-legged on the porch. An outdoor carpet covered rotting planks that sagged under my weight. It must have been years since anyone had changed the carpeting, because the wiry thistles were flattened into a slick surface. In some places, there were gaping holes. Mason had flown to Bristol, Tennessee, four hundred miles east of Nashville, to work at the drag races that weekend. I planned on driving to Bristol on Saturday night so that I could spend Sunday afternoon watching the Thunder Valley Nationals from a television production truck. We'd drive home together. Until we both returned, Free Love had put catching Dawn on hold.

"The fleas will keep coming back," Joan said.

An obese Chihuahua named Mama trotted up the middle of Sycamore Street. She had recently delivered a litter of puppies. Her swollen teats swung inches above the pavement. Mama lived with Bernice's neighbor Millie Cleary. I'd met Millie once and only for a few minutes. She was a retired factory worker who spent her afternoons patrolling the neighborhood. She was big-boned and imposing. Bernice mentioned her name so often in conversation I knew she relied on Millie for advice. But what kind of advice was Millie giving her?

A gray, scrawny cat named Blackberry followed Mama. He licked his paws whenever the dog stopped to sniff a mailbox, plastic grocery bag, or beer can. The cat sneezed up huge tendrils of green pus and breathed with a heavy rasp.

Bernice had her own cat, but she also fed a lot of the neighborhood animals. Like clockwork, these cats and dogs visited her porch each afternoon to get whatever treat she kept in her Tractor Supply Company bag. In the coming months, I'd meet more and more people who were just like Bernice and Tray. They rarely had enough money for medical bills or groceries, but they always found a way to share a plate of food with a neighborhood stray. Their kindness changed my first impression of Sycamore Street. It might have looked dirty and mean, but a profound generosity underscored this neighborhood.

Mama and Blackberry jumped on the porch, gave the puppies a quick once-over, then sat near Bernice's feet. She scooped Kibbles 'n Bits onto two paper plates and handed them out. Blackberry and Mama ate from their respective plates without stealing the other's food or acting possessive about their own. In fact, none of the dogs and cats I met on Sycamore acted aggressivley toward each other, and 99 percent of them liked humans. They weren't healthy, but they were socialized and relatively happy.

"I can transport Mama to the Fix Foundation," Joan offered.

"Millie sells her puppies for twenty-five bucks apiece every six months or so. She said I could do the same with these here." Bernice gestured at the sleeping litter.

My eyes flitted toward Joan. She worried about the Magic 8's future as much as I did, mainly because of Bernice. Bernice had an extraordinary amount of influence over the puppies. And since Millie influenced Bernice, she did, too. Dogs are considered property in Tennessee. Legally, since they were born on Bernice's property, she owned them. She could kick us off her porch and sell those pups to whoever wanted them. Bernice was a kind woman with childlike qualities, but those same qualities made her impressionable. She listened to whoever's voice was the loudest, and Millie exuded the authority of a high school principal. Besides weather and fleas, now we had to worry about an uninformed busybody getting in the way of the Magic 8's safety.

A scruffy terrier mutt named Eddie tromped through the yard. He arrived minutes after Mama and Blackberry. I never saw Eddie's house or family, but every day he stopped by for his plate of food. Eddie jumped on my knee with uncontained excitement, tail flapping back and forth, tongue licking any part he could reach. I patted his head, then gently pushed him away. Like every other animal on Sycamore Street, he was sick. Eddie looked healthy from maw to rib cage, but scabs covered his haunches. It was pretty obvious he had mange.

Until I hung out on Sycamore Street, I didn't realize that having a healthy animal is quickly becoming another middle-class privilege. None of the dogs lived in fences. None were spayed or neutered. Most had some sort of illness, and they all had fleas. Millions and millions of fleas lived on Sycamore Street. Bites covered my shins, arms, and ankles. I even found them on my stomach and back. Whenever I'd hung out on

Bernice's porch and returned home, I would avoid our front door and enter through the basement. I would strip off my clothes, dump them in the washer, and jump in the shower before I touched any of our mutts. I often daydreamed about lowering a dome over Sycamore Street and annihilating every flea and tick. We would spay, neuter, and vet every dog and cat before we lifted it back up.

"I keep telling those people Eddie needs to go to the vet," Bernice said.

"Well, now, Bernice, I think Eddie has mange. Don't you? That's another reason the puppies staying here for too much longer is dangerous," Joan said.

If I ever needed to negotiate, I'd want Joan by my side. Joan's southern accent made her words sound so musical they softened her blunt but honest opinions. Once, we had been waiting at the vet's office with one of our foster dogs, Rosalie Aprile. A woman asked when Rosie would be up for adoption. When Joan inquired after the woman's own dog, a woolly beast sprawled over the tile floor, the woman answered she wanted "to get rid of this thing." Joan replied, "Then you aren't the kind of person we'd allow to adopt our dogs." The woman didn't answer but sat there with a confused smile, like she wasn't sure what she'd just heard. Mason said Joan's voice was like maple syrup on burnt pancakes. By the time anyone bit into them, it didn't matter that they were ruined because it'd been so sweet getting there. She was the perfect person to deliver bad news because it took people so long to figure out if they should be offended or upset by what she said.

"If you take her babies, Night won't come back," Bernice said.

"That's not necessarily true," Joan answered. "She was here before she got pregnant, wasn't she?" She waited until Bernice nodded, then continued. "I think the puppies should stay with their momma as long as possible, don't you?" She paused again, waited for the nod. "But the fleas are going to continue being a problem. The vet said fleas could even *kill* them."

The word *kill* stung. I'd only known the Magic 8 for ten days, had only spent a few hours around them, but thinking about them dying sent waves of maternal nausea through my stomach. The puppies were supposed to distract me from Joe and his impending death. *They* weren't supposed to die. Puppies didn't die. They played and napped and ate and exhaled their enchanting puppy breath. With every ounce of brainpower, I willed Bernice to say yes.

She wore her usual attire: a sweatshirt, sweatpants, and sandals with socks. She acted frazzled and repeatedly looked over her shoulder, as though she were hoping that Millie would be making her rounds. Her resolve was weakening.

"Some of these puppies might not make it. I just want to make sure you're prepared for that," Joan said.

I wanted to scream that *I* wasn't prepared for that, but I kept quiet because I didn't want to gang up on Bernice. I also didn't know her well enough to gauge her temper. I didn't know how easily or how often she got offended. She might ask Joan to leave if she got angry enough. But if I stayed in Bernice's good graces, we'd still have a shot at saving the Magic 8.

"Now, I want you to know that *whenever* we take those pups, we won't give up on Night," Joan said.

"When would you want to take them?" Bernice asked.

"The vet says they can eat soft food at a month," Joan answered. "That's two weeks away."

Bernice stayed quiet for a few anxious seconds, then said, "If you can't catch Night by then, you can take her babies."

I exhaled. Two weeks was a long time for eight puppies to survive on Sycamore Street, but it was the first time Bernice had wavered since I met her on the greenway.

As though our conversation had summoned her, Dawn stood across the street.

"Right there's Night," Bernice said.

She sounded excited, as though Dawn's presence was an honor. Every time Dawn showed up, Bernice acted the same awestruck way. At first, I had thought she was acting like a teenager who saw an idol. But on that porch, I realized her feelings about Dawn were much more personal, because it involved a relationship. A few years ago, a friend had told me about a doe who visited her backyard each day. Eventually, that deer ate from her hand, and that interaction, that rare synthesis between something so wild and a human, made her feel singular. That's how Dawn made Bernice feel. She made her feel special, as though Dawn saw something about her that nobody else could.

Bernice mixed up another plate of dog food and laid it on her stone walkway. Dawn assessed the porch for a solid minute or two, then approached. My pulse quickened. She stood fifteen feet away. It was by far the closest I'd ever been to Dawn. Before she started eating, she pointed her slick black nose at her litter, but they were all sound asleep, exhausted after their latest bath. She didn't acknowledge Mama, Blackberry, or Eddie, and they didn't acknowledge her.

Joan and I didn't move, didn't twitch an eyebrow, because we knew she'd bolt if we did. Unlike a lot of strays, Dawn didn't eat in a hurry. Instead, she frequently paused and scanned her surroundings, aware at all times of any movement. Often, her gaze rested on her puppies. After a while, one of them roused, probably because she sensed her mother, and started whining. One after another woke, until that mass of fur was thirty-two pink paws, sixteen ears, and eight tails wiggling and worming. Finally, they were all whimpering for their mother.

"Does she eat here every day?" Joan asked. She sounded excited.

"Every single day," Bernice boasted.

"What if we drug her?" Joan asked.

11

Only in the Movies

A wall of fifty television monitors glowed, washing the dimly lit production truck in fluorescent radiance. Every screen displayed different scenes at the Bristol Motor Speedway. In the pits, girls dressed in chaps handed out car wax coupons or subscriptions to hot rod magazines. Fans wearing John Force baseball hats meandered through the midway, eating corndogs and drinking beer. Crew guys wrenched on engines under awnings splashed with advertisements for motor oil and antifreeze. On the racetrack, top fuel dragsters flew down the quarter-mile strip at speeds of 300 miles per hour. They accelerate faster than a space shuttle. Even inside the truck, we felt the cars' vibrations, each launch approximating a small earthquake.

The temperature was boiling outside the production truck, but inside it was a dry sixty-eight degrees. The engineers kept it that cool for all the electrical equipment. The television crew consisted of sixty-plus people who were spread all over the racetrack and communicated via headsets or radios. Live sports production has its own vernacular. Phrases like "take six," "roll gold," "track red," "shade twenty-one," and "real-speed replay" buzzed through the truck. Out of the nineteen people working inside the remote studio, two were women. I was one of them for fifteen years.

I texted Nancy. *How's Joe doing?*

I'd brought Miss Annie with me, and Nancy was watching the rest of our pack. She promised she'd call if anything happened, but it was my first overnight trip in months. I felt guilty about leaving Joe. Nancy didn't answer right away, so I put my phone away.

Miss Annie and I sat in the back row, so that we were out of the way. Miss Annie observed all the energy and chaos like she understood it. Being inside a production truck wasn't new to her. Before we had adopted Joe, Annie traveled with us to all twenty-four races. Afterward, she had gone to at least half. The crew, many of whom had left their own dogs at home, treated her like our mascot. Our satellite engineer had even made her an official National Hot Rod Association credential with her picture on it. Someone occasionally walked through the truck and whispered *hello*. Annie licked their hand if she recognized them. She ignored them if she didn't.

Live television production is the definition of organized chaos. When it's done well, it's the ultimate example of teamwork, because it involves individuals working under pressure on separate tasks that all funnel toward one product, the television show. Sometimes, shows are smooth and events unfold as predicted; but in live sports, particularly racing, unpredictable events can change everything. These events normally mean weather conditions or competition upsets, but occasionally they're more challenging. Twice, we saw racers die—Darrell Russell in a top fuel dragster and Scott Kalitta in a funny car. Both times, regardless of the unfolding tragedy, we had produced a television show for thousands of viewers.

I didn't leave my job because I didn't like the work. My job was challenging and exciting once I arrived at the television compound; but in order to make a middle-class living in sports broadcasting I needed to travel a lot. That meant being away from my pack. When Joe started losing his mobility, Mason and I had lengthy discussions, all of them leading to the same conclusion. It was time I got off the road. We both strongly felt we owed it to Joe to be there at the end. It meant cutting our income by half and living on a shoestring budget, but it also meant Joe wouldn't die alone.

Nancy responded to my text during first-round eliminations. *I hate to tell you this, but Joe's suffering. It's time.*

Those words went down like hands down a barbed wire fence: scratching, ripping, and slicing the whole way. Sometimes, it takes someone else to point out what we already know. Mason and I had known for weeks that we needed to make the call, but we'd kept putting it off because we wanted Joe to die on his own. We didn't want to make the impossible decision to euthanize him. I thought about Mason's conversation with Nancy—the one that always ended with "only in the movies." Joe could exist as an invalid for months, but existing wasn't living. Joe wasn't going to improve. He wasn't going to have another day of eating strawberries in the sunshine. There were no more excuses. We had done everything we could to make his final months comfortable, but it wasn't enough. We owed him one more thing. Wasn't this part of loving an animal? I read Nancy's text again. *It's time.*

* * *

The drive from Bristol, Tennessee, to Cedar Hill is five hours and consists of mostly long black stretches along Interstate 40. Inside the headlights' glow, the dotted lines stretched and then dissolved into the pavement. Mile marker after mile marker passed, ticking backward as though counting down time. It was late on a Sunday night, so the traffic wasn't heavy. I'd offered to drive, but as always Mason insisted he'd do it.

Mason was tired but in a good mood. It had been a solid show, and he was high from it. I didn't want to bring him down, so for a couple hours I didn't tell him about Nancy's text. I waited until we drove through Knoxville, until the city's haze rose above the tree line and broke through the darkness. Mason and I had seen so many of those orange-pink glows before. We had watched the sunrise over the Great Salt Lake, driven through a lightning storm in the Mojave Desert, and woken up next to the Snake River in Idaho. We'd traveled from one end of the country to the other multiple times by plane and car. We had a trunk-load of real-world experiences, but we'd never lost someone we loved like Joe. Our family had never been tested before, not emotionally.

Mason and I had only dated for a year before adopting Joe. We'd spent so much of our married life with him that I wondered how our family would change after he was gone. Because it *would* change us, that much I knew, and I desperately wanted it to stay the same. I thought about my tattoo, the symmetry of the initials *m3jd*. I thought about how the *j* glued both ends of the formula together. I finally had the family I'd dreamed about as a young girl, and I was already losing them. It isn't fair that our time with animals is so short, but it's a fact, and on that car ride I confronted it head-on. When my mind quieted, and the only sound was the night rushing through our windows, I told my husband about Nancy's text. He didn't say a word, but he held my hand the rest of the way home.

* * *

I started working before dawn the next morning. I didn't check my email or turn on my cell phone. I didn't want any distractions. Daybreak was the stillest time in our house, the only time when all the dogs were quiet. I got more writing done in the day's first hour or two than I did in the rest of it combined. Miss Annie was the only dog who had crawled out of bed with me. She tiptoed into my office, nestled in her dog pillow, and fell right back to sleep. But even with the quiet, I couldn't work. All I could think about was Joe.

An hour later, I heard Mason start the coffee pot, use the bathroom, brush his teeth—the normal sounds of his morning routine.

Finally, Miss Annie's ears perked up. Mason stood in the doorway.

"I called Dr. Dan," he said.

He wasn't looking at me when he said it. He was looking over my shoulder at a Mother's Day card taped above my desk. That year, Mason had bought a card specially designed for dog parents, but he altered it. He had printed out individual pictures of our six mutts and taped them over the original cartoon figures. Corny but endearing expressions were already typed underneath each picture. Under Joe's photo, the caption read, "No bones about it, Mom, you're dog-gone great!"

Joe's fur was still thick and scruffy in his picture. A tree had fallen across the creek, creating a natural bridge too flimsy for people but perfect for animals. Joe stood on it, tail mid-wag, nose dirty and tongue hanging out, as though he were smiling. Joe had always been the happiest in the woods. I imagined him sprinting across the forest floor, pushing faster and faster, without an ounce of fear. I imagined the pure joy he must have felt when he ran through the woods. It was the one place where I had no control over him. Even my most forceful call, the one filled with urgency, couldn't get his attention.

"He's coming Thursday morning."

My body tensed until I felt as though I might splinter. I wanted to say, *No, cancel the appointment.* I wanted to say, *We could wait until next month, when you're home more.*

"It's time, baby. He's hurting," he said.

I looked at Miss Annie, but she was already watching me, as though she knew I needed her. She understood. She always did.

12

EUTHANIZING JOE

A cluster of goldfinches fluttered across our lawn and landed on a magnolia branch. A hummingbird hovered over the hydrangea bushes we'd planted in front of the house that spring. The young flowers drooped in pink and purple bulbs. Our neighbor was bush hogging. His tractor rumbled back and forth across the field, churning out a tail of ragweed and brush. The cicadas, crickets, and frogs chanted from the forest. Their song grew louder as the shadows stretched farther across the grass.

The world around us acted as though it was a normal summer evening, yet for our family it was anything but normal. Normal would have been taking Joe for a walk on the greenway or a swim in Sulphur Fork Creek. Normal would have been giving him a bowl of dry dog food, and a biscuit for dessert. But by this time tomorrow, Joe Poop wouldn't be here. He wouldn't walk, swim, kiss, eat strawberries, or dig for sweet potatoes ever again.

Even what we were eating wasn't entirely normal. I rarely ate meat, but tonight we were grilling steak because it was Joe's last meal. Mason slapped the New York strip on the hibachi we used for tailgating. Joe lifted his nose and inhaled the scent of sizzling steak. He was sprawled across his dog bed. My contribution to dinner was a pound of strawberries. I offered one to Miss Annie, but she snubbed it. Dessie chewed the fruit, then spat it out. They were holding out for the steak, so Joe Poop and I shared the whole bowl while we waited.

My emotions swung from one end of the spectrum to the other. Since we'd gotten home from Bristol, Joe hadn't been able to stand without help, let alone walk to the water bowl. It was time for Dr. Dan's visit, and it had never been so clear before. Yet, at times, I felt wildly angry at the unfairness of watching a creature we loved as much as a child, die. Then, gratitude overwhelmed me, gratitude for meeting Joe at all. *M3jd*, that special formula tattooed on my shoulder, symbolized the first time in my life that I hadn't felt worthless or unlovable. It was the first time I felt *needed*. And it was all because of those dogs.

We finished the steak as the evening turned blue. It took a lot less time than finishing the berries. Mason and I laughed a lot. We reminisced about the highlights of Joe's life: chasing deer through the woods, sprinting after seagulls at St. George Island, trotting across Baltimore's Inner Harbor, hiking in the Pocono Mountains, walking through Times Square, watching *NCIS* with his dad, swimming in Sulphur Fork Creek, and, of course, winning the title of "Best Kisser in Nashville."

Sometimes, I caught myself daydreaming about Joe dying on his own, even dying right then on that porch on that perfect summer evening. I wanted his life to end on his terms. When the futility of these thoughts overwhelmed me, tears poured unchecked. During those moments, I'd stick my face near Joe's snout. He'd kiss away my tears with the same firm but gentle touch I'd known for years. That's when I said my goodbye, in one of those emotional swells. I whispered I loved him, and I'd never, ever forget him.

The next morning, early dawn, Mason carried Joe from his bed to the blankets we'd spread on the living room floor. I locked the pack, except for Annie and Dessie, on the deck. I completed the final preparations for Joe's death like I swept floors. I didn't think about what I did. I just did it. Dr. Dan stopped by our house on his way to the office. He told us we were doing a good thing. He promised it wouldn't take long.

And it didn't take long. It didn't take more than thirty seconds.

Back then, I thought euthanizing an animal was the worst way to say goodbye. I wouldn't realize until much later that being able to say goodbye is a gift.

* * *

Mason and I drove to Centennial Park after we dropped Joe Poop's body off at Music City Mortuary. The air was already brutally hot. We walked one lap around the Parthenon, changed course, and backtracked to the flower garden. A multitude of sprinklers rained over colorful petals. I grabbed Mason's hand. We took off sprinting through the garden and cold water soaked our T-shirts. We laughed and cried all at the same time.

13

MEADOW, FIRST–TIME FOSTER–FAILURE

A thick carpet of leaves crackled under my hiking boots and made it difficult to distinguish the footpath from the forest floor. Nobody had used our trail since last spring. It was winter, five months after we'd met Dawn, five months since Joe died. Meadow Soprano walked beside me, standing at my thigh. Her feathered tail swooped back and forth. She walked proudly: nose lifted, ears raised. Once in a while, she'd bound a few steps ahead or linger behind for an interesting smell. Like Joe, she acted more alive in the forest. Mason called the woods a canine version of Disneyland.

A soft wind carried the scent of a burn pile smoldering at H&M's sawmill a quarter mile up the road. The mill workers' chainsaws buzzed and cleaved. Their front-end loaders rumbled over the muddy ground, lifting bundles of wood from one pile to the other. These sounds were reassuring. I liked being alone, the luxury of getting lost in my mind; but I also appreciated knowing somebody was within reach.

Our house perches on a bluff that slopes toward a dry creek. Meadow suddenly bolted down the creek's spine. Yellow and brown leaves sprayed behind her. She liked exploring, but she always kept me in sight. We had fostered Meadow twice before we adopted her. The first time, she had lived with us for a brief two weeks before a housewife who home-schooled three children adopted her. Free Love took all the precautionary steps to ensure the family was the right fit. Joan interviewed the husband and wife twice. I interviewed them once. We had called their personal references and visited their colorful, cluttered, artistic house. Everything implied they were the perfect fit, but things hadn't worked out.

A "forever family" is a phrase people use because the alliteration of the *f* makes it sound good; but it isn't always the truth. For whatever reason, every so often, dogs are returned. We had dogs who were returned because they shed too much and others because they showed aggressive tendencies. In Meadow's case, it was anxiety. In her new house, Meadow had torn up the family's shoes, toys, craft projects, and books. They said she had pooped or panted pools of drool all over their carpet. They had tried working with her for months, but she never improved. In fact, she only got worse. The behavior they described was so out of character with the way she had acted at our house that, at first, I was annoyed. But the second time she lived with us, we discovered something none of us could have predicted. Meadow suffers from separation anxiety when she's not around other dogs. She needs to live with a pack.

Mason had fallen in love with Meadow the first time she lived with us, so he couldn't say no the second time. I didn't argue for several reasons. For one thing, Meadow is an exceptional dog in both temperament and appearance. She's a combination of a Great Pyrenees and German shepherd, wearing the long blond-white tresses of a Pyrenees with the unmistakable black snout of a shepherd. She's as gentle as the former but as protective as the latter. Most importantly, she fit in with our pack immediately, as though she belonged with them. She respected the elders, played with foster mutts, and walked on the greenway with the confidence of a dog who was loved since birth, not one who was abandoned in a trailer park. Sometimes, she even reprimanded foster dogs who chewed on furniture or got too close to candles, just like Joe had. Maybe that's another reason I didn't argue about adopting her. In so many ways, she reminded me of Joe.

But I also didn't push back because the timing was right. During Meadow's second stay, we had known Joe wasn't going to make it more than a few months. His absence meant we'd have the resources to invite another animal into our family. For us, it wasn't about replacing one dog with another. It was about the number of animals in our community who needed homes. When Mason and I moved to Robertson County, we'd made a pact. If we had the resources, we shared it with homeless dogs, and at that time we had room for Meadow. Besides, I knew Meadow *wanted* to stay with us. The way she had acted in her last home versus the way she acted at our place confirmed it. It was like she picked us.

As though she'd heard my thoughts, Meadow stopped in mid-prance, flipped her head over her shoulder, and waited for me to catch up. We were winding through a part of the trail we'd named Bat Cove because of the abundance of bats that lived in the cedar trees.

Back in 2003, when Mason and I first saw our house, we hadn't been impressed. We thought it was an unremarkable brick home: fourteen hundred square feet, three bedrooms, two baths, and an unfinished basement. Plus, it needed a lot of work, including pricey items like a new roof and windows. But our opinion changed as soon as we walked the property line, which extended for seven acres through the woods. It was the perfect space for dogs.

We had three goals during our first few weeks in our new home: build a chain link fence around the yard, install doggie doors, and carve a trail through the forest. Eventually, we replaced the roof, windows, gutters, hot water heater, and doors. We built a deck, ripped out the carpeting, and installed tile and hardwood. However, all the indoor improvements had waited until we finished the fence and the trails. Our dogs were always our priority.

We didn't own a tractor or a riding lawnmower, so making the trail hadn't been easy. Armed with gloves, rakes, shovels, hedge clippers, and a chainsaw, Mason, Joe, and I cleaved, plowed, scraped, and sawed our way through an overgrown forest. It was man, woman, and dog versus the earth. Joe's favorite job was digging out stumps, a talent he later used for sweet potatoes in the garden. His second favorite task was walking the trail. One of the quickest ways to make a footpath is to walk on it, repeatedly. Joe and I had tramped lap after lap around our property line.

Our home's isolation was part of its appeal. My office window faces north. I can see one house light shining at night, but it's so far away it looks like a pin. One neighbor lives two hundred yards to the east, and another lives one thousand feet to the west. A bush-hogged field with a tobacco barn sits across the street. We can see the closest house only when the trees are bare, but in the spring and summer the forest encloses our home until it feels as though we are cocooned in a green cloud. When we had first bought the house, we both spent over a hundred days a year on the road. The bustle of hopping from twenty-four different cites, airports, hotels, time zones, temperatures, and racetracks made our secluded home the perfect place to retreat and recharge.

Meadow leaped from the creek bed onto the bank. Her hair ruffled in the sunlight. She trotted to the firepit, and sniffed the ashes and then the kindling stored under a blue tarp. For a split second, out of the corner of my eye, I thought I caught a glimpse of Joe's salt-and-pepper fur. I looked behind me. I knew he wasn't there, but I looked anyway because he felt *so real*. Joe's presence was the most intense in the woods. Sometimes, on those trails, his memory was so strong I heard the clinking of his tags or caught a whiff of his fur.

I've lived with more dogs than humans for almost two decades, and I've learned a lot from them. Some are simple concepts, like stretching several times a day or napping in the sunshine. But some are more complicated, like how to forgive and how to love without restraint. Two of the most complicated concepts Joe taught me were how to intentionally live in each moment and how to draw out experiences by utilizing my senses; and he taught me to do both in the woods. Because of him, I started hearing the calls of owls, woodpeckers, bats, squirrels, turkeys, and frogs. Joe showed me beehives, birds' nests, and fossils, and once he even pointed out a raccoon skull wedged into a tree. He reminded me to smell the wild honeysuckle when it bloomed, the creek when it ran, and the warm rain as it blew in from the south.

I'd felt grief before we lost Joe. My grandfather passed when I was twelve. We lost both of Mason's grandparents when we were newlyweds. A handful of personal friends have died over the past decade or two, some tragically. But none of those experiences prepared me for how much I wanted one more day in the woods with Joe. The need reminded me of being a little girl and wishing the stuffed animals on my rocking chair would start talking. I knew they wouldn't, but that didn't stop the wanting. At some point, I understood that want might never go away.

As I watched Meadow meander to the trunk of an old sugar maple and slurp long and hard from the bole, I thought about the last lesson Joe had taught her. The sugar maple's base split into five arms and created a basin that held rainwater for weeks. The previous winter, Joe had led Meadow to the trunk. He looked frail standing next to her, but she matched his old-man, wobbly pace with patience. He demonstrated how to stand on the tree's root and lap from its deepest parts. He drank for a long time, and took an even longer time crawling back out of the bowl. There were three more of them along the trail, and he had taken her to each one. These lessons were the most precious relic I had left of Joe, as symbolic as my tattoo.

Suddenly, something heavy crashed through twigs and brush behind us. At first, I wasn't sure what was running toward us and tensed, but then I saw two does galloping thirty yards away. Their retreating tails were stark white against a sea of tan and gray trunks. Meadow's body went rigid. She brandished her tail and whipped it back and forth in two deliberate motions. She took a step forward.

"Meadow," I called, sternly.

She faced me with an expression of incredulity, and made a sound somewhere between a bark and groan. But she waited for the deer to pass. It wasn't easy. She flexed every muscle in her body—even her paws seemed pointed, as though she stood on tiptoe—but she stayed put. Sometimes, she was so different from Joe. Joe would have completely ignored me and sprinted after the deer. Then, he'd have taken his time getting home, examining every scent he missed during the chase. We were lucky if he showed up two hours later. On his longer deer hunting excursions, even when the creek ran dry, Joe returned soaking wet and matted with briars. He always found a swimming hole.

For a split second, I missed the sparkle in Joe's eyes when he ignored my command. I missed watching him fling his body forward through space, completely unafraid. His abandonment had always reminded me why being alive felt so good. Then, I thought about how many hours I spent waiting for Joe to return: worrying he had gotten lost, had been attacked by a coyote, or was stuck in a trap. Joe's wildness may have been exhilarating, but Meadow's obedience was comfortable and safe.

Meadow and I listened to the leaves flatten under our weight. I imagined the loamy scent of her paws; they would have reminded me of Joe's. Meadow pushed her head into my palm, seeking confirmation that she'd done the right thing: the thing I asked her to do. Meadow has a supernatural ability for reading body language. Somehow, through an unconscious gesture, she had recognized my initial disappointment, and it confused her. I tapped her head. She smiled. Bits of silt stuck to her tongue. Her tail thumped the air. After half a lap, Meadow swerved off the path. She stuck her snout into an obscure pile of dirt and twigs and huffed. She had already forgotten our encounter with the deer.

PART II

14

A Split-Second Decision

Mason, Miss Annie, and I went canoeing on the Red River shortly after we moved to Robertson County, ten years before we met Dawn. The river's name comes from the color of its mud, an orange-brown mixture as thick as clay. Our research said the slow-moving currents were perfect for a lazy day of floating. We packed sandwiches and a six-pack of beer in a cooler, and stuffed towels, books, and clean clothes in a dry bag. We rented canoes from Red River Rentals in Adams, Tennessee, who said the trip took four to five hours. They loaded a group of us in a bus painted like tie-dyed shirts and dropped us off eight miles upstream. We'd land at the same place we parked.

The afternoon started exactly as planned. We occasionally paddled but mostly just drifted. We saw a herd of deer grazing in a pasture, snapping turtles sunbathing on half-sunken snags, a groundhog standing outside his cave. A heron posing on spindly legs fished in shallow water. A red-tailed hawk swooped above the river's surface, hunting for a rodent in the greenery lining each bank. We passed farms with cows drinking from the water, glided under a bridge with an arching trellis. Honeysuckle filled the sultry air with its sweet fragrance. Blackberries also grew wild, but most were already ripe. Handfuls had fallen off their stems and left deep purple blots on the rocks.

Miss Annie curled up in a pile of towels I'd arranged on the dry bag. She occasionally stretched or licked my hand. She seemed perfectly happy. Miss Annie loved sunbathing, and lay in the sun all year round. When it was too cold outside, she napped in squares of sunshine on the wood floor. But Annie wasn't a swimmer. I had introduced her to water when she was a puppy. We were hiking along the Potomac River in Virginia on an August afternoon. At some point, I flipped off my hiking boots and stood ankle-deep in the river. I held Annie where she could feel the water lapping against her undercarriage. She spent thirty seconds in the river before she lurched out. She never liked water, even back then.

I can't say exactly when Miss Annie rescued me from my self-destructive path. It didn't happen right away. I acted as worthless as I felt for the first six months she was in my life. At that point, I hadn't talked to any family member in years. I was engaged to a successful satellite engineer, but it was a meaningless gesture. He cheated on me; I cheated on him. I dropped out of a master's program with one semester left. I didn't have a dime in the bank, but I didn't have anywhere to go anyway. I was terribly lonely.

Slowly, ever so slowly, Miss Annie changed me. She needed me, and her need filled me with a sense of worth, a reason for being. There's a saying among dog lovers so popular it's printed on T-shirts and posters. It says, "I strive to be the person my dog thinks I am." That cliché piece of wall art hangs in my house because it reminds me of Miss Annie. Her stubborn, unrelenting love gave me the courage to admit bad decisions, such as staying engaged to someone I didn't love or surrounding myself with people as emotionally damaged as me. She gave me the courage to change, *to want* to change. I often wonder whether I could have fallen in love with someone as stable as Mason if I hadn't met Annie first. She made me a better person because she believed in me.

I slid over the gunwale a few times and floated down the river for a few hundred feet, but I was the only one who got in the water. Mason had grown up flipping burgers at the neighborhood pool, but chlorinated water was the extent of his experience. In time, he would get over his fears, and eventually snorkel off the coast of Culebra, Puerto Rico; but back then he wasn't a confident swimmer. He always worried about what lurked underneath him.

Mason paddled from the stern. He worked outside and sported a farmer's tan. His chest was pale while his arms were brown, lean, and muscled from running cable up and down a quarter-mile racetrack. His chest never tanned. It didn't burn, either, just stayed winter white. I liked that Mason worked outside, that he came home covered in dirt and sweat. I liked his callused hands and pasty chest. Men who worked at desks or wore suits had never appealed to me.

We snacked on apples and nuts, drank a beer, then two more. By the third hour, I could tell Mason had a buzz, but so did I. His hazel eyes, normally so clear, glowed red and glassy. The river split around a small island and merged on the other side, funneling back together in a narrow straightaway. Before the funnel, the currents were calm, almost tranquil; but they drastically changed in the merge. We weren't prepared for it. Sun-and-beer drunk, bordering on drowsy, we hit rough water.

Ripples were the only sign of the river's strength, but I noticed them much, much too late. The water yanked the canoe and we capsized. The current's strength felt as powerful as an ocean's riptide. The canoe's bright red keel scooted past me, but it barely registered. I didn't consider that we were losing our only mode of transportation. I wasn't thinking about the clothes, books, cooler, beer cans, and sandwich bags littering the bottom of the river. I didn't even think about Mason. Miss Annie was my only concern. For a few frantic seconds, raw terror vibrated through every particle in my body.

Mason emerged first, twenty feet downstream. Annie's tiny head popped up in the opposite direction, right in the heart of the rough water. I can't think of a better way to define the term *split-second decision* than that exact moment. I was faced with the choice of helping my husband or helping Annie. Sure, I thought about it, but in retrospect my reasoning was biased toward Annie from the start. In less than a second, I rationalized Mason was taller and had a chance of touching the river's bottom. He wasn't a strong swimmer, but he could swim. Even with all this rationalizing, my gut reaction disregarded my husband for my dog. It was as though I didn't have a choice. I silently told Mason I loved him and turned toward Annie.

Miss Annie's black eyes glowed with terror. She wildly kicked, but she didn't have enough physical strength for fighting the currents. I couldn't hold her because I needed both hands for swimming. Instead, I positioned myself behind her, surrounded her with my arms, and created a breakwater against the current. Annie acted as though she'd been swimming her whole life in those calm waters between my arms. Once she stood all four paws on dry land, I started searching for Mason. He reached us first. He came slogging through the foliage, barefoot but baseball cap still on his head.

The first thing he asked: "Is Annie all right?"

Miss Annie stood by my feet shivering so hard that she seemed as though she might crumble. With her hair soaking wet and hanging flat, she looked like she weighed three pounds, an overgrown rat or a skinny Chihuahua. To me, she never looked more beautiful. I didn't know what to expect when I found my husband—maybe anger, or at least annoyance. But Mason acted as though it had never crossed his mind I'd do anything but help Annie first. The pecking order was always clear.

* * *

I was shopping for dog food one day during that summer we were chasing Dawn. It had been almost ten years since we capsized our canoe. I passed several racks holding collars, training leashes, vitamins for joints, brushes for long or short hair, shampoo for hot spots, and life jackets. I paused, backed up. The dog market has exploded over the past decade. Stores now sell items, such as life jackets, specifically for canines that weren't easily available or popular when we first moved to the countryside. The yellow, orange, and red vests ranged in size from extra-small to extra-large. The larger ones looked suspiciously like the human version. I picked up the tiniest one, examined the buckles, and read the tag. A picture of a Yorkshire terrier modeled it. Miss Annie's canoeing days had been long over by then, but I bought it anyway.

15

BENADRYL AND PUPPIES

Bernice and I picked out four puppies: two black; one white; and the fattest, who wore brown splotches on his fur. They were three weeks old. Their eyes were open but still slightly cloudy. The black ones acted alert, but the other two slumped against my chest, as though they were exhausted. A flea scurried down the white blaze of fur between the biggest one's eyes. Another scampered across the folds of his muzzle, then tunneled farther into his coat. A third flea leaped onto my arm, sunk his saw-like teeth into my skin, and sucked blood. I'd soon have a bright pink mark added to the darker ones already lining my arms. It'd only been a few days since their last bath, but the pups were already flea-infested and filthy. We needed to catch Dawn *today,* before it was too late.

Bernice and I placed the dogs next door in front of an empty house with several eviction notices pasted on the door. Joan had formulated a much more sophisticated plan for catching Dawn on our third attempt. It still involved baiting her with puppies, but it also included drugging her with Benadryl. We finally realized we were up against a far wilier animal than we'd anticipated. A vet had recommended putting three Benadryl in a hot dog. He warned us not to feed her anything besides the meat because too much food might counteract the pills. The Benadryl wouldn't knock her out, but it would make her sleepy. Mason was working out of town, but I promised I'd text him when or if we caught her.

Joan had also enlisted the help of Springfield Animal Control because they owned resources we didn't, like a catchpole and a net. A catchpole is a five-foot rod with a vinyl-coated release cable at the end. The humane society calls this device a control pole. If used properly, we'd snare her without getting bit. We planned to catch her, using the pole or net, out in the open while she was groggy and tending to her puppies.

Free Love's original intent had been to house Dawn and her pups with a foster family who owned a barn, but I volunteered for the job days after Joe died. I rationalized I needed a big project. Taking care of eight puppies meant I wouldn't have time to think about Joe or, more importantly, his absence. Also, I didn't want to deal with death again so soon, and I was worried that if we waited much longer some of the Magic 8 wouldn't make it. Joan repeatedly warned that the puppies might not survive, but I needed them to live. Death had shadowed our house for so long, and I wanted to replace it with life. Puppy life.

An officer from Springfield Animal Control pulled up next to Bernice's house. I'd been to the animal control office multiple times, but I'd never met Tawanda. She was a completely unexpected but welcome surprise. The officers I knew were all middle-aged and white, but she was a thirty-something Jamaican woman who wore dreadlocks and talked with a thick Caribbean accent. Her attitude was different, too. Instead of the nonchalant, seen-it-all-before attitude I normally encountered, Tawanda cooed over the puppies and listened to Dawn's story with interest. Meeting her only bolstered my confidence.

Dawn showed up across the street several minutes after the pups started crying. She stood next to an overgrown hedge. The sun was high overhead, shadows at a minimum; but as usual, it took me a second to see her.

"She's here," I said.

We tried acting as casual as possible. Bernice lit a cigarette. Joan and Tawanda debated whether to use the net or catchpole. I sipped my green tea, but every nerve in my body strained toward Dawn. All those days of hanging out with Bernice on the porch had paid off because Dawn felt comfortable enough to move closer. Bernice said Dawn had eaten the pills over an hour ago, but I didn't notice any visible signs of drowsiness.

The puppies' whimpers rose, reaching zeniths of need. Dawn's ears strained toward their cries, zeroing in on their location, as though she was trying to understand how they ended up in such a strange place. Finally, she approached her puppies. Dawn nuzzled them for a second before the fattest latched onto her nipple. His priority was clear. She let him drink for a moment before plopping down onto her side. The others immediately scrambled for a teat. Finally, she rested her head on the ground, as though she planned on napping. It was exactly what we hoped would happen, what we *needed* to happen.

We waited for a few anxious minutes, minutes that felt like hours. We waited until we all agreed she felt relaxed. Until we all looked at each other and nodded in understanding. We were a ragtag group: a southern belle, an unemployed housewife, a middle-aged activist, and a Jamaican dogcatcher. We barely knew each other; but in that moment we were a team bonded by one goal: catching Dawn.

Watching Dawn on the gravel driveway, I knew that catching her was as critical as saving the puppies. She wasn't as physically weak as they were, but she was emotionally battered. If only she could hear my thoughts. If only she could understand my language, then I could tell her that I only wanted to help, that I wanted to show her what it felt like to live without fear. What it felt like to experience the kind of love that made saying goodbye to Joe so hard. I willed my thoughts at her, as though somehow if I thought about it hard enough, she'd be able to read my mind.

Tawanda grabbed the net and started toward the abandoned home. She walked slowly, almost on tiptoe, circling around the house's rear. Her movements were deliberate, as though she was trying to minimize any sounds. No breeze ruffled the air, but even so, she approached Dawn from behind. I felt a surge of confidence, and to Tawanda's credit, she made it within a few feet before Dawn sensed her. The mutt lifted her snout and sniffed the air. It was now or never. If Tawanda waited any longer, Dawn would be gone as quickly as she appeared. I silently yelled, *Throw it.*

As though she heard me, Tawanda took one more step and lobbed the net. It sailed high over Dawn's head and landed directly on top of her. *We had her.*

And then we didn't. We didn't have her at all. Just like every other time, my hopes swung from joy to defeat within seconds. Before I could even stand, the net was empty. People say if there's a hole in a fence, a dog will find it, and Dawn proved them right time and time again. In the one second between when the net touched her and Tawanda yanked the cinch cord, she had slipped out.

Dawn sprinted toward the street, ears alert, tail rigid. Three of the pups had immediately tumbled off her nipples and started screeching; but the biggest still clutched onto one. He hung from her belly and sucked with all his might before he finally dropped to the road and rolled a few feet.

Bernice whispered, "I told you animal control ain't worth nothing."

Joan didn't need to say a word. Disappointment flashed in neon across her face. It mirrored my own.

* * *

We came so close to catching Dawn on our third attempt that we decided to try again using the same tools, Benadryl and puppies. The only difference was Mason was helping, and animal control wasn't. Tawanda said her boss wasn't keen on letting her spend another afternoon chasing a feral dog. In retrospect, it wouldn't have mattered if Tawanda helped anyway because Dawn turned on her heels the moment she saw us.

"Let's follow her. Maybe she'll pass out somewhere," Mason said.

The Benadryl didn't knock her out, but it visibly affected her. We'd upped the dose with an extra pill. She acted woozy, and occasionally she shook her head, as though trying to snap the fog out of it. But she knew we were tailing her and kept looking back. She didn't break into a sprint but trotted at a steady speed. Her body was as thick and wide as a bull-dog's. Her teats hung to her knees and swished back and forth. Carrying that much milk must have been painful; but she never stopped moving.

We tracked Dawn onto an adjoining block, then the next one. We watched her cross porches, cut across yards, and dodge behind fences, as though every step was preplanned. Dawn knew her neighborhood, but Mason and I were in foreign territory. Finally, she stopped in front of a white house with pale blue shutters. Impatiens in decorative pots blossomed in pink and red on both sides of the front door. Unlike every other place on the block, the yard was mowed and uncluttered. Dawn watched us move closer for less than a second, and then she simply vanished behind that tidy house with blue shutters.

We scoured a four-block radius; we searched in drainage pipes, abandoned buildings, and dumpsters. We asked everyone we passed if they knew her. Several people recognized the dog we described. Some even called her by different names—like Bear, Flash, and Shady—but none had spotted her recently. They all confirmed that she'd been roaming their area for more than a year, and that nobody could get close enough to touch her. Someone said a neighbor fed her daily, which explained why the Benadryl hadn't made her groggier. It also explained why a street dog bordered on plump. However, it didn't explain her fear of humans. If so many people fed her and cared for her, then what was she so afraid of? Why wouldn't she let anyone touch her?

Mason and I decided we'd cover more ground if we split up. We agreed to meet at Bernice's house in an hour. I searched for thirty minutes before I ran into a man sitting on a lawnmower chained to a trellis at a church-sponsored halfway house. He wore overalls and swished flies from a mug of beanie-weenies. I introduced myself, and told him I volunteered for Free Love. He said his name was Jimmy. I asked if he'd seen a black dog with swollen teats.

"Do y'all mean Blaze? he asked.

Jimmy said he had known Blaze for eighteen months, since she was a pup. Jimmy stood over six feet tall, and talked with a soothing cadence. Before long, his southern twang and slow-motion mannerisms charmed me. I found myself wishing I had all day to listen to his stories. He had such a calm demeanor that I understood why dogs liked him. He said Blaze grew up at the old bus terminal with her mother, Heinz, and a sister he called Biscuit. Jimmy explained how the previous year he had been buying a hundred pounds of Dog Chow a month at Tractor Supply Company to feed that pack of strays. He boasted they would line up "military-style" on the other side of the carport as they waited for him to pass out their bowls.

I asked Jimmy if he had ever touched Dawn. He leisurely waved away another fly, then looked me square in the eye, as though he was sizing me up. I felt like he was asking me to make a pact, or maybe he was testing my mettle, wondering if I could handle what happened to dogs in his part of town.

"No, but she been abused real bad," he said.

"By who? The neighbors?" I asked.

"Ma'am, it ain't my neighbors."

"By who then?"

"By the police," he answered.

According to Jimmy, in June 2013, Dawn's pack was roaming between Cheatham Street and Sycamore Street. Animal control had tried capturing them but weren't successful, so they called the cops. The Springfield Police Department showed up with shotguns and chickens. They set the birds loose in the deserted field behind Jimmy's halfway house. When the pack started chasing them, the officers opened fire. Jimmy said he heard dogs screaming long after they stopped shooting. He said it took them a few days to kill them all: all except for one. Dawn was the only dog who survived the massacre.

16

Repercussions

The humidity pressed against my skin. Sweat trickled from my nape to my bra strap, and soaked my stained T-shirt. The sun seared my shoulders. Bernice must have started a tomato plant at some point because it stood next to the rusted trellis. Its leaves hung limp. Mama rested on blankets pushed against the house and panted with her tongue hanging out. She'd been napping in that spot most of the afternoon, yet she acted like she had just sprinted a mile. The heat was brutal and inescapable, just like Jimmy's story.

Mason looked as sweaty as I felt. Neither of us had seen Dawn since we split up. Joan and Bernice were cleaning the puppies with baby wipes. While we'd been searching, they fed them mush, a concoction of puppy formula and wet food. It was the first time they'd eaten anything besides their mother's milk. The chunky taupe mixture stained their snouts, ears, paws, tails, and bellies, as though they'd bathed in it, but there wasn't a drop left on the paper plates.

I'd only heard Jimmy's story an hour ago, but the magnitude of it crushed me until I couldn't keep it to myself anymore. Inhaling deeply, I shared it with everyone on the porch. I started slowly, describing Jimmy and the halfway house, and then finally recounted his memories of that day in the field: the day the police shot a pack of dogs. Joan's hands, a second ago lovingly swabbing the puppies, stayed frozen. Bernice lit a cigarette. Mason listened with his head down, arms crossed, defensive, as though protecting himself. Nobody said a word when I finished.

I didn't want to believe Jimmy's story, but an insistent nagging said it was true. I'd read the Tennessee code, Title 44, concerning dogs a few years ago and knew it included leash, fence, and muzzle mandates. But Title 44 also defines animals as property, meaning they had as many legal rights as a mattress or a credit card. How could I expect our local cops to act with compassion when our state describes animals as property?

Besides the fact of our archaic laws, Jimmy's story seemed credible because of the abundance of strays. If a pack hadn't been running on Sycamore Street, then the police wouldn't have shot them. And packs of strays weren't rare in Robertson County. Over the years, I'd heard more than one horror story about dogs attacking children and killing domestic animals.

I hadn't known about the extent of the animal overpopulation problem when we first moved to Robertson County, but it didn't take long before we noticed how many dogs roamed free. Many looked well fed, wore collars, wagged their tails, and appeared perfectly happy to be sunbathing, chasing cars, or tearing up a McDonald's bag tossed out of a car window. But as time passed, we began noticing other dogs scavenging alongside roadsides and through parking lots. These animals were sickly and scared. And it was easy to understand how they ended up banding together for survival.

One of the reasons for the ongoing overpopulation problem is that not many people spay or neuter their animals. Before I had started fostering dogs, I assumed the only reason my neighbors didn't get their animals fixed was the cost. At a regular vet's office, it can be several hundred dollars. There are a few low-cost spay and neuter clinics within twenty-five miles of Springfield. But for people living off of food stamps and disability, fifty dollars can break monthly budgets.

Although cost is part of the reason, Joan had opened my eyes to another problem: a deep-seated cultural complication. She said that people didn't get their animals fixed because they thought castration meant deprivation. I thought she was stereotyping; then one day I listened to a bearded man wearing mud-stained work boots tell Dr. Dan he wouldn't neuter his two-year-old Rottweiler because it would alter Harry's masculinity. I had wanted to challenge that hardworking man, but I kept quiet because it would have accomplished nothing, except maybe lead to an argument. My feelings about my community often hover in the same uncomfortable, ambivalent zone I experienced that afternoon in Dr. Dan's office. I consider Robertson County my home and have close friends who own homes, attend school, and work here. Yet it's also a place with some deep-rooted Old South customs that I sometimes find frustrating, even infuriating.

Mason finally broke the silence. He said he didn't think it was legal to open fire in a neighborhood without a threat, no matter what the socioeconomic level. Bernice said she would have heard the shots. Joan pursed her lips and looked up at the sky. I could tell that, like me, she believed Jimmy's story.

"I'm going to have to stop by the police station and find out if they really did this," I said.

"They ain't going to tell you even if they did," Bernice said.

"They didn't do it," Mason said.

It was so hard for my husband to distrust authority. That inclination comes easy for me because of growing up with such unreliable parents. But Mason grew up with a mother and father who taught him that morals and manners were as important as love. I often teased him that his family was like a modern-day version of *Little House on the Prairie*, minus the prairie. His parents had divorced when he was six, yet the split was so amicable they lived two houses apart from each other for years. Mason came from a background where doing the right thing was normal, so believing that our local law enforcement could sanction such blatant cruelty was impossible.

Before we left that evening, Bernice said, "I think you should take this puppy here; he ain't feeling good."

Four of the Magic 8 went home with us that night. The next day, Bernice asked us to take the rest. Nobody could escape the weight of Jimmy's story. When I loaded the last of the litter into the backseat of my car, I felt mixed emotions. The Magic 8 were finally going to live somewhere safe and clean, but Bernice might be right and Dawn might never come back. She might disappear, like Heinz and Biscuit, and all the other dogs that died in a field behind a halfway house.

Jimmy's story stung at first, but the real horror came later, when I had time to process it. I was deeply conflicted. My idealistic self wanted to side with Mason, but an insistent nagging kept asking why Jimmy would make up such an unbelievable tale. Conflicted or not, I couldn't post anything on the Farnival until the police department confirmed or denied Jimmy's accusations. In college, I'd trained as a journalist. The instinct to verify such an outrageous story before writing about it had been pounded into me. Asking an official wouldn't be easy, and as Bernice said, they'd probably deny it; but I had to ask. I had to ask if they'd massacred a pack of dogs behind a halfway house.

17

Behind a Halfway House

From the carport of the First Baptist Church halfway house, I had a clear view of the untended field where Dawn's fear of humans crystallized. It was the length of a football field, a sea of washed-out green-and-beige weeds. Spots of color from Styrofoam cups, soda cans, potato chip bags, and shattered brown glass emerged the longer I stared. I held a white-and-blond puppy in my arm. I had brought the one I named Adriana to meet Jimmy.

The halfway house stood to the left, small and efficient, with brick walls and a tin roof. Middle-aged men, men as ungroomed as that field, sat in lawn chairs under the carport's shade or strolled the length of the driveway. All those men were in purgatorial temporary housing, on their way from one life stop to another. Dawn must have felt like she was in purgatory, between a before and an after, on the last day she roamed in that field with her pack.

The men acknowledged Adriana with a nod or a smile. One asked if he could hold her. When I put her in his arms, he beamed. I felt satisfaction knowing that puppy had the same effect on those hardened men as she did on me. She was a dose of happiness in one furry handful.

"Is Jimmy around?" I asked.

"Ain't seen Jimmy, ma'am."

I hadn't seen Jimmy in a few days, either. However, I couldn't stop thinking about how he bought one hundred pounds of dog food a month for a pack of stray dogs. He had so little, but he gave so much. Just like with Bernice, I felt a deep sense of admiration for his generosity. Jimmy had disappeared shortly after we pulled the puppies from the bramble patch. Rumor was he'd moved back in with his girlfriend. Rumor was he'd started drinking again.

I thanked the man for his time, then turned back to the field. Eight dogs had been chasing chickens on the day Jimmy stood right where I did. Afterward, there had only been one. Imagining that scene, one that included thundering gunshots and bloody dogs, was hard enough; how hard was it to witness? How helpless had Jimmy felt? Had he been able to numb his emotions or had he felt every shot?

The day after I heard Jimmy's story, I took Joan to the halfway house to meet him. It was the last time I saw him. I asked him why he thought Dawn had survived. He said she had probably hidden in a drainage pipe. He'd never seen her crawl into one, but he had seen her crawling out. He was sure about one thing, "That dog can vanish." One second, she'd been chasing chickens with "Ol' Heinzy," and the next she was gone. It took the police a few days to kill all the dogs, and Jimmy said he hadn't seen her that whole time. He had just assumed she was dead.

Beyond the field, I saw the metallic rims of the drainage pipes glimmering at each intersection. I'd never noticed how many of them existed before I started searching for a stray dog with a black coat. As frustrating as it was when we were trying to catch her, I knew her dark fur and crafty fear had saved her life in that field. The metal pipes were the perfect hiding spot for medium-size animals, particularly ones with Dawn's coloring. If she had crawled deep enough inside, the police never would have seen her, even if they'd searched. She would have blended in with the blackness. I imagined Dawn hunkered down inside the pipe's innermost workings, melded into the nucleus, invisible except for her glistening eyes. Between each gunshot, human voices would have sounded:

voices that Dawn didn't forget or forgive. It was easy to understand why she wouldn't let anybody touch her.

Eventually, I gathered up Adriana, waved goodbye to the men at the halfway house, and nodded toward that field, as though I owed it some sort of salute, as though a battle had been fought there. Somehow, I knew I'd never see Jimmy again. But as I drove away, I thought about everything I'd tell him if I did.

Most importantly, I'd tell him that what he witnessed in that field wasn't meaningless. His story had saved Adriana's life and all seven of her littermates. They weren't going to die in a bramble patch or from a flea infestation. They weren't going to get shot by police, and it was all because of him. I'd tell him that one day his story might save Dawn, too.

18

THE WESTMONT

Miss Annie and I moved to Nashville, Tennessee, from Virginia almost thirteen years before I met Dawn. We rented an apartment near West End Avenue and lived within walking distance of Music Row, Vanderbilt University, and Centennial Park. Eventually, Mason moved in with us, but for the first six months it was just Miss Annie and me. I fell in love with the city's west side mainly because of Centennial Park. The park hosted the 1897 World's Fair and commemorated the occasion by building a full-size replica of the original Parthenon. The building still stands at its center. In the warmer months, Centennial holds art festivals and musical events. It hosts big band dances on Saturdays, when hippies, musicians, and intellectuals groove under a pavilion. Family-friendly movies are shown on weeknights. On Sundays, people gather at a flagpole for a drum circle. Dogs are welcome at every event. Nashville was the first place I lived that I didn't want to leave.

Mason and I rented an apartment at a quaint establishment called the Westmont, primarily because it was cheap. In 2000, the West End was changing. The homes that lined the streets, some of which were antebellum, were being sold to companies that would eventually tear them down and replace them with cookie-cutter townhouses with overpriced rents. The Westmont hadn't been renovated in years, but it was one of the last bastions of affordable housing. It was shaped like a square. A pool, grills, and picnic tables sat inside the perimeter. There were also designated grassy areas for animals to do their business.

I met my first friend in the pooping section. Bo Burr was a twentysomething hippie who worked in a sound studio and had a boxer called Buddy. One evening, Bo invited me to his next-door neighbor's apartment, but he warned me dogs weren't allowed. Buddy had never been allowed past Yaz's front door, and they'd been friends for months. He explained that Yassir Hakim was from Saudi Arabia and "didn't *get* dogs." I was offended at first. How could I be friends with someone who didn't *get* dogs? I planned on spending thirty minutes there at most. I ended up staying for two hours.

* * *

Yaz stopped by my apartment one afternoon a few weeks after we'd met. He'd made checking in on us a daily habit. Miss Annie sat in her dog bed with her snout lifted, nose working overtime because the aroma of steaks on the grill at a nearby restaurant floated in through the open window. A neighbor played a guitar on his porch two floors above us, occasionally breaking into song. Another of the reasons I loved Nashville was because live music was everywhere, even right outside our door.

Yaz sat on the couch and started talking about his day. He didn't acknowledge the six-pound dog curled up five feet away. I'd never met anyone who didn't melt around Miss Annie, but he was impervious. To be fair, she didn't acknowledge him either; but she had always been a snob, so her behavior wasn't that strange.

Yaz studied electrical engineering at Vanderbilt, wore wire-rimmed glasses, and had slightly crooked front teeth. His hands moved in sweeping gestures when he talked, as though he conducted his conversation. Conversations with Yaz were boisterous, entertaining, and always leaning toward humorous. He found humor in everything. I liked him so much that sometimes I forgot he didn't *get* dogs. When he sat, he looked taller than five feet ten, because his knees reached his chest. He wore sandals, baggy jeans, and a T-shirt. He often pushed his glasses up his nose with his finger, particularly when he laughed. He laughed a lot: a rumbling, contagious belly laugh.

We talked about everything and anything during those afternoons. We discussed general topics like current events, world news, and politics, but we also talked about more personal subjects, like his religion, roommates, professors, classes, and his latest electrical invention. He swung his arms wider and talked faster when he discussed his inventions, family, or friends. I could tell he cared more about those three things than anything else.

That afternoon, he was sharing a story about how his roommate almost got mugged scalping tickets outside a Phish show in St. Louis. As he explained the details, he became more energetic than usual, so energetic that even Miss Annie noticed. Or at least she couldn't pretend not to notice. Suddenly, she stood up, trotted to the couch, and sniffed Yaz's sandal. It was the first time she'd shown any interest in him at all.

Yaz dropped his arms to his knees, and stopped talking in midsentence. His eyes widened. He was as still as I've ever seen him. I realized he wasn't impervious to Annie, but he was unsure around her. I finally understood what Bo meant when he said that Yaz didn't *get* dogs. But I also wondered if it was a personal choice or a cultural one. Everything about Miss Annie was new to him because dogs had never been a part of his life before. Until he came to Nashville, he'd never seen one in a house. In his town, dogs were mangy strays who scavenged in trash piles. They sure weren't little snobs who slept under the covers and ate mashed sweet potatoes from the same fork I did. Annie took her time investigating his foot, scrutinizing each toe individually.

When she was satisfied, she leaped on the couch, a giant leap for a six-pound dog, and Yaz gave a rumbling laugh. Annie plopped on a cushion two feet from his arm, as though she sensed his approval. It was a bold move. Yaz stayed quiet for a beat more, and pushed his glasses up his nose, as though he was trying to figure out how to sit next to a dog, because that was as close as he'd ever been to one. Then, as though not missing a beat, he continued with his story about his roommate scalping tickets.

Miss Annie had a way of making people feel special. She didn't give out her affection easily. She withheld it just long enough so that people started wondering why the cute little dog in the room didn't like them, and people always wanted her to like them. I saw it time and time again. Nobody was immune to her charms. From rugged bikers to grandmothers, from southern good ol' boys to educated northerners, from toddlers to the elderly: she made them all smile.

When Miss Annie finally returned people's attention, they acted as though they had won something special, something coveted. A lot of the fascination had to do with her size; but Annie's likability factor went beyond her appearance. She was the rare combination of a little dog who didn't yap. She was playful but liked being quiet. She never demanded attention; in fact, she shunned it. Mostly, she acted happy as long as she could keep her eye on me.

Miss Annie stayed next to Yaz until well after dark. Before he left, Yaz said that the next time I stopped by his apartment I should bring her with me. Annie met my surprise with a look that said, *What did you expect?*

* * *

One afternoon, Annie and I were walking across the Westmont quad. Our apartment complex had a small laundry room on the basement floor of the building diagonal to ours. We were on our way to switch a load from the washer to the dryer. Annie followed at my heels with her tags jingling their reassuring, familiar chime. Her ears rotated like miniature satellites toward any new sounds, and her nose gleamed with a damp sheen. Yorkshire terriers are traditionally photographed with long hair, but I never let Annie's grow more than a few inches. She preferred it short, and acted annoyed when it trapped leaves on her underbelly. If it got too long, she'd spend hours picking twigs from her stomach and legs, then catch my eye with an expression that said, *See what I have to go through?* When it was shorter, like on that day, her silky hair developed a soft wave, a tousled crown of amber and black.

From twenty yards away, we saw Yaz standing in the shallow end of the in-ground pool. His arms were raised in conversation, and he held a red solo cup. I noticed he was having trouble balancing it while he talked. A gold liquid sloshed over each side. His laughter, twice as cheerful as normal, confirmed he wasn't drinking water. It was after six. Miss Lettie, the fifty-year-old office manager, floated on a raft next to him. Every month when we dropped off the rent, she would give Miss Annie a biscuit. She wore a T-shirt over her bathing suit and curls that looked like they'd been set in the 1980s with hot rollers and hairspray. She held a can of Coors Light. The Westmont didn't have as many rules as the new townhouses popping up around us. Management allowed booze and dogs in the pool area, but no glass, which seemed so reasonable that everybody obeyed.

I didn't know if I was more surprised that Yaz was drunk or that he was partying with Miss Lettie.

"Ahhhhh, Miss Annie," Miss Lettie said when she saw us.

Yaz shouted out Annie's full name. "That's Miss Annie Daisy Banana Fanny!"

Miss Annie heard him. Actually, the whole quad probably heard him. Annie bounded to the pool but stayed a safe distance from the water. She vigorously wagged her tail in greeting. As we walked away, I heard Yaz slowly pronouncing her full name. He said it as though confirming someone so small deserved such a royal name.

Over the next two years, Yaz and Annie became so close he occasionally took her for a ride to Vanderbilt. She never left me willingly, so Yaz had to carry her to his car. But every time they returned, they both radiated health and happiness, as though spending time together was good for both of them.

One day, Yaz asked if he could take Annie to campus. It had become so normal that I didn't even wonder why. I must have assumed he was dropping off a paper or checking a grade. He asked again the following day, then the next. Three times in one week seemed so excessive that I finally said, "What's up?"

He confessed that the same pretty girl who had ignored him for the last four years actually talked to him when he had Miss Annie.

"She's a babe magnet," he answered.

* * *

Annie bolted down the hallway and skidded to a stop outside Yaz's apartment door. She twirled on her back paws. Yaz had just graduated. He'd been my closest friend in Nashville for two years, and pretty soon I'd have to say goodbye. In a few weeks, Mason, Miss Annie, and I would drop him off at Nashville International Airport. He'd spend two days traveling home to Saudi Arabia. He told me he'd come back to visit, but we both knew he wouldn't. Yaz's family wasn't wealthy, and plane tickets to the United States weren't cheap.

Besides, things would be vastly different when he returned home. Saudi Aramco, a Saudi Arabian oil company, had funded his Vanderbilt education on the condition that he come back and work for them after graduation. Yaz would keep his promise and work in the desert for years. He would also keep his promise to his family and marry a woman he met for the first time on his wedding day. He would integrate back into Middle Eastern culture as easily as he integrated into ours.

Yaz's apartment was always packed to capacity with an eclectic crowd. He was rarely alone. On that afternoon, a white guy from Kentucky, a molecular biologist from Long Island, an Israeli musician, and three Middle Eastern students circled the living room. They were smoking a hookah and speculating about returning to the Middle East after 9/11. The students hadn't been home since the planes hit the Twin Towers. On West End Avenue, Yaz and his friends were insulated from the growing animosity toward Muslims, but they wondered how that would change once they left Vanderbilt.

Bo's dog Buddy had been sleeping on the floor under the TV and barked when he saw Miss Annie. Buddy was finally allowed past the front door, but he wasn't allowed on the furniture or in the bedroom, kitchen, or bathroom. He was basically regulated to the space between the couch and the television. In retrospect, Buddy hadn't been the best dog to introduce to a person who admittedly grew up in a family that considered dogs filthy creatures. Buddy drooled, panted, farted, burped, snorted, and knocked over furniture within the first five minutes of meeting anybody. He didn't have a manner in his entire muscular body.

Miss Annie didn't approve of Buddy, either, but he adored her. He tried nuzzling her, but she instantly did an about-face and stuck her tail in his snout. She let him sniff her rear end, then trotted away, oozing contempt. Yaz had made Miss Annie a special place on the sofa and piled pillows three feet high, so that she could be at the same level as the rest of us. Yaz scooped her up and plopped her down on the top pillow. She threw Buddy a glance, twirled a few times, then settled into her favorite noodle position. Miss Annie knew precisely where she was allowed and Buddy wasn't. She also knew that, in Yaz's house, she was queen.

* * *

Yaz knocked on my apartment door the afternoon before he left. He gave me a prayer rug and three Santa Claus stamps as farewell gifts. I've never used the stamps, and have them tucked away at the back of my sock drawer with my other precious mementos. Annie pirouetted at Yaz's feet.

"Can Annie come hang out while I finish packing?" he asked.

"I'll go get her leash," I replied.

"She doesn't need it," Yaz said.

"Are you going to carry her?" I asked.

"She'll come with me," he responded.

Mason raised his eyebrows. "She won't leave Mel," he said.

Yaz said, "Come on, Miss Annie."

At first, she didn't move but tilted her head one way, then the other, as though trying to figure out what he meant.

"Come on, Miss Annie," he said again and tapped his thigh.

Annie looked at me—a quick goodbye glance—and then pranced, tail high and wagging, out the front door. After a few moments of shock—and, yes, jealousy—tenderness swelled inside me. Miss Annie had changed Yaz; but he had changed her, too.

19

DAWN UPDATES

Dawn still hadn't returned twenty-four hours after we'd pulled the Magic 8 from Sycamore Street. However, suggestions poured in when I wrote on my blog about our third and fourth failed attempts to catch her. Many sent recommendations we'd already tried, like baiting her with food. But some ideas were unique and creative enough for us to do follow-up phone calls or Google searches. Justin from Topeka, Kansas, proposed using a tranquilizer gun, which sounded like a grand idea. Joan called veterinarians all over middle Tennessee and Kentucky, and finally located a gun at the Nashville Zoo. It took them a few days to return our call, and by the time they did we'd already nixed the plan, because of a solider named Tim.

Tim was stationed at Fort Campbell in Kentucky and wrote to us about a similar stray who had lived outside his base in Iraq. He said that she'd delivered three litters before he decided to do something. He had used a tranquilizer gun, hoping to catch her and get her spayed, but he'd failed, terribly. He explained that shooting a dog with a tranquilizer dart wasn't as easy as it sounds. The shooter had to hit an exact location or she could die, like the stray had in Iraq.

Geoff from Brentwood, Tennessee, recommended hiring a cowboy who knew how to use a lasso. Joan and I researched local ranchers, and left numerous voicemails. Finally, one cowboy called back and said he'd never roped a dog before, but he'd give it a try. When I posted the idea on the Farnival, a woman named Ruth from Seattle emailed me about the downfalls of lassoing a dog. She said roping a cow was one thing, because their necks were so big, but yanking that hard on a dog could snap its neck. She'd seen it happen. Back then, I didn't put a lot of thought into what it meant when readers tried helping us catch Dawn. Now I realize that without them having cared enough to write, we might have hurt or killed her. In some ways, that vast invisible universe of readers was as much a part of her story as anyone on Sycamore Street.

I used the same photo for all of Dawn's updates that summer. I only had one. Scraggly weeds cover the foreground; a Styrofoam plate of Kibbles 'n Bits sits on the far left. Dawn is walking along Bernice's concrete pathway. Her head hangs inches from the pavement. Her shoulders slump forward and her spine dips at the middle, maybe because her swollen teats hold five extra pounds of milk. Her silhouette looks remarkably similar to an old workhorse with swayback. Mud covers her too-dainty paws. She's mid-stride, tail glued to her hind legs, with only the very end curving outward. In that picture she looks exhausted, like she's too tired to keep moving.

I posted what would become my last Dawn update for over a month in late June. I explained that Bernice hadn't seen her for twenty-four hours, not since we pulled the Magic 8, and quoted her text: *Y'all think she'll come back home now that her babies are gone?*

Back then, if anyone told me that I wouldn't care when I found out the answer, I wouldn't have believed it.

20

Blossoming

We introduced Pippi and Tory, our two foster dogs, to the greenway's swimming hole on a brutally hot morning. Pippi and Tory lived with us during that whole summer we chased Dawn up and down Sycamore Street. Mason and I were drenched in sweat after fifteen minutes of walking on the greenway. The dogs must have felt like they were moving through stew, with air so thick it held weight. Before I lived in Tennessee, I'd heard comments about how slow southerners move and always assumed it was another cliché. But since relocating, I've discovered there's a lot of truth in it, too. Their speed doesn't have anything to do with intellect; it's a physical necessity.

Sara and Meadow sprinted straight to the creek and bounded into the water. Droplets rained down around them. Tory meandered as far away as her leash allowed and began eating grass. Pippi crept to the water's edge and sniffed. Pippi and Tory had been in Free Love's care for months and lived in several different foster homes, but they still weren't ready for adoption.

Sometimes, Joan moved dogs from home to home because the families became too attached, but other times she did it because the animals had special needs. Pippi and Tory were inordinately shy and needed socialization training. They had come a long way from when we first met them, but they were still nervous around everyday outdoor things, like bicycles, skateboards, strollers, storm drains, mowers, and the creek we walked beside every morning.

Sulphur Fork Creek runs through Robertson County for ten miles and weaves along the greenway for two of them. When it rains, the creek rushes. And when it pours, the banks flood. But it hadn't rained for days. Pippi tapped her paw against the slow-moving surface, then jumped backward, like it might retaliate. She waited a beat, stared intently, and finally realized nothing was going to happen. She sniffed her paw and cocked her head. Her already enormous ears were at full attention. It must have been the first time she'd been that close to a large body of water.

Pippi was about a year old, weighed forty pounds, and wore a plain beige coat with a consistency somewhere between wiry and soft. Everything about her appearance was plain, except for her ears. Her ears were extraordinary. They were as big as her heart-shaped head and stood upright with the very tips slanting down. Nancy's teenage daughter Charlotte had edited a split-screen photo for the Farnival. She juxtaposed Pippi against Dobby, a beloved house-elf in the Harry Potter books. The similarities between their ears was so striking that Joan published the picture on Petfinder.com. Pippi would eventually get adopted because of that photo. Her future family, a couple from Gallatin, said they had grown up with the Harry Potter books.

Tory, a medium-size heeler mix, was our other foster dog that summer, and the only canine who acted completely nonchalantly about the water. Tory ate grass or dug in the orange-brown dirt. Tory was also wary, but her wariness extended to people. She didn't run from us like Dawn, but she never acted comfortable, either, as if she couldn't let down her guard around humans. Tory never cuddled on the couch or sought our attention. She didn't wrestle or play with the other dogs, at least not when we were around. Once, I heard her playing with Meadow on the porch and walked outside. I caught a glimpse of her salt-and-pepper coat and playful stance before she noticed me and stood rigid. She stared so hard it became clear she was analyzing my body language, as though she expected a reprimand.

I recognized her behavior instantly because I did the same thing in uncomfortable situations. As a child, I had learned the importance of observing body language because my father's volatile behavior demanded it. I studied the tone of his voice for sarcasm, irritation, or amusement. I noticed his facial expressions and posture, whether his skin color was drunk red or pasty sober. His hands were within eyesight at all times. Tory acted the same way around us, but recognizing it didn't mean we knew a magic cure.

From experience, I understood lack of confidence was partially to blame for the dogs' wariness. Not all of them were physically broken, but across the board they were emotionally banged up because, at some point recently in their lives, they had been stressed about everything, from food to safety. This trauma manifested itself in many different ways, but aggression and insecurity were the two most popular repercussions. We fostered dogs who snapped over things like bed space, rawhides, or toys. A mutt named Bentley had lunged for the inner thigh every time we passed another dog on the greenway. Mason and I still have scars. But we also met animals like Pippi, who was so timid she treated a slow-moving creek like a defendant in a murder trial. For the most part, these scared dogs often shed unwanted behaviors once they lived in a safe, structured environment. For others, it took a lot more time and patience.

I waited for glimmers of self-confidence in every stray who walked through our front door. It was the moment when I checked their name off my mental list of rescued dogs. I didn't consider housing, feeding, basic training, or finding them homes—all legitimate parts of the process—as important as inciting those first sparks of self-esteem.

Most of the strays who arrived at our house rarely exhibited any singular characteristics. But when they consistently received food, exercise, and affection, they morphed into individuals with personalities. I called this transformation *blossoming* because it reminded me of watching my dahlias bloom each year. Once that bud busts through the dirt, it's like there's no limit to what it can become. The stalks grow tall, sometimes five feet, and wide, sturdy enough to support hundreds of colorful petals crammed onto weighty heads. When I saw those anxious mutts become as vivid, bold, confident, and original as a dahlia, I knew they were going to be fine.

Pippi watched the water lap the creek bank for a full five minutes before she pulled toward the paved trail.

* * *

The next day we stopped at the creek again. Pippi acted the same cautious way she had before. She tapped the water and investigated her paw. She cocked her head, but instead of standing back, she stepped forward so her front paws were submerged. I didn't make a single motion. If anything, my body froze, but inside I cheered. I glanced behind me and caught Mason's wide smile. He felt as triumphant as I did.

Pippi scrutinized Meadow until it became obvious they were communicating through body language. Meadow was standing knee-deep in the creek. Her long blond hair was so lush and full that it made her look ten pounds heavier. She wanted Pippi's attention and thwacked her feathered tail against the water. Pippi stared but didn't budge. Meadow tried a different tactic and dipped her head completely underwater. She emerged shaking from ears to tail, water drops spraying six feet around her. Several sparkled on her snout. She was begging Pippi to play, but Pippi wasn't having any of it. Meadow was always beautiful, but on that day she looked singular. I felt a keen sense of pride that we had adopted her. I'll never understand how anyone had abandoned her, but selfishly I was grateful.

Pippi shifted her focus to Sara, who was swimming laps from the pedestrian bridge to the creek bank. Sara had learned how to swim from Joe. She had watched him jump in everything from mud puddles to the Atlantic Ocean before trying it. Once she did, she swam like a natural; however, unlike Meadow, who thought water was just for games, Sara took swimming seriously. We only saw Sara play in water once. Six years before Joe died, Mason and I had piled our dogs into a rented minivan and driven to St. George Island on Florida's Gulf Coast. We'd stayed for a week at a townhouse overlooking a leash-free, dog-friendly beach. Joe and Sara had galloped down the coastline for seven straight days.

Pippi watched Sara gliding through the water, but didn't move beyond her comfort zone. I wasn't surprised. I'd noticed her stubbornness the day she moved into our house. She had walked through the gate in our backyard, sat down, and for days downright refused to come inside. She'd never even ventured into the basement. Instead, she stared through the chain link fence as though she wanted to be anywhere else. It wasn't easy, but I ignored her. I let our pack demonstrate that she was in a safe place. And eventually, it worked. One day, she followed Meadow through the doggie door and popped into our kitchen with an expression that echoed my surprise. Since then, she'd been making slow but steady progress.

We didn't know anything about Pippi's past. On a frigid January morning, someone had found her sleeping on the doorstep of the local pharmacy without a collar, tags, or a chip. But we did know about Tory's past. Tory had been born in Lincoln County, Kentucky, another rural farming community an hour northeast of Springfield. Four dogs were in her litter, and her brother Buddy was the first one who Free Love fostered. Free Love only helped dogs outside of Robertson County if it involved an extreme situation of neglect or abuse, and the Lincoln County litter qualified for both. They came to our attention when a Farnival reader named Beth wrote to me. I had asked her permission, changed names, and then posted her email on the blog:

May 5, 2014

Melissa: Be forewarned: This email will make you angry. I know that I'm angry. My son, Timothy, had a pup that was attacked by a littermate. The dog was separated from the pack in order to heal. After it was better, the dog was allowed to run free, and it was hit by a car. Since then, the dog's leg has improved. A week or so ago, something attacked the dog. He now has only about 4 inches of tail. What tail he does have looks horrible. I nearly vomited when I saw it.

The stub is bare and is various shades of red and black. My son has called animal control to pick up the dog.

I don't need a dog and cannot afford to have one, but I know the dog will be mistreated if he is put in a shelter. I called a vet who said that tails are hard to heal and suggested that we cut it off. I told my son that I'll pay for the tail surgery and getting the dog neutered but I need time to build a pen.

I'm angry that my son created this disaster. By the way, the dog's name is Buddy and he's a timid fellow. My husband agrees that we don't need an animal and cannot afford it, but that compassion should win out over convenience.

Thanks,

Beth

Beth worked ten-hour shifts cleaning college classrooms, took a class a semester, and lived in a singlewide trailer. Her husband was an assistant in a home for disabled people. She drove a car with 300,000 miles on it and could barely afford her own monthly bills. Yet she paid for Buddy's neutering and to have his tail removed. Like Bernice and Jimmy, Beth is one of those heroes nobody ever hears about; one of the people who sacrifices their own needs to care for an animal. Eventually, Free Love got involved and found homes for Buddy and his littermates. Tory was the last dog from the Lincoln County litter.

* * *

Three days after Pippi discovered the creek, she charged into the water, dove underneath, and sprang back out, wearing a smile as big as her ears. As though the water was a drug and she was high, she acted electrified. Soaking wet, she sprinted back and forth along the bank, kicking up a trail of mud. At one point, she lost her footing and rolled into the creek, performing such perfect somersaults that it looked practiced. She reached deep water and a panic crossed her eyes while she slashed her paws up and down in a chopping motion. It was a bizarre way to swim and proved that swimming wasn't programmed into a dog's DNA. Somehow, she made headway, gained her footing again, and resumed her crazy yet beautiful water dance.

All of this happened within seconds, while I stood stock-still with my mouth hanging open: surprise, pride, and accomplishment all mixed together and swelled inside me like some inspiring chorus. Pippi had blossomed. She was as original and colorful as any dahlia. No one who witnessed Pippi's behavior that morning would have believed that she wouldn't sip from the creek three days previously. Even Meadow stood stunned, unsure about the rules in this new game.

"What the—" Mason said. Laughter choked off his words.

Once I heard his voice cracking, I started laughing and couldn't stop. We laughed until our rib cages ached, until we couldn't catch our breath. Our hysterics only inflamed Pippi, who continued acting as though the creek was the best invention since air-conditioning. Those were the moments that made up for every Lincoln County litter we heard about. We gave those dogs safety, but they gave us laughter.

Pippi walked back to the car with a newly confident stride. She held her snout as high as her tail and didn't cower when a teenager sailed past on his skateboard or a family cycled toward us. A path of wet paw prints trailed her. The largest pad formed the shape of an upside-down heart: four matching ovals spread evenly around the bottom. Her prints looked etched into the asphalt, as though they were permanent, as though the dog who made them knew exactly where she traveled.

* * *

A year after we stopped fostering dogs, I waited in a hotel room in Chandler, Arizona. I was expecting a ride to Phoenix Sky Harbor International Airport, where I'd take a direct flight home to Nashville. I'd been ready to leave for an hour, but had thirty more minutes before my ride left for the airport. I always woke up early on travel days because I couldn't wait to get home. It seemed fitting that for the first eighteen years of my life, I'd never wanted to be home; now, I didn't want to be anywhere else. My view consisted of two palm trees and miles of brown sand. The landscape's neutral coloring reminded me of Pippi.

I pulled my computer out of my carry-on and opened the Farnival website from a folder labeled FAVORITES. I typed *Pippi* in the search bar. Twelve posts appeared. I clicked the one titled "Pippi Loves to Swim." Mason had edited a video of Pippi playing in Sulphur Fork Creek and added a circus-themed soundtrack. In the background, I hear our laughter. The camera occasionally pans past Tory chewing on grass, Meadow wading in the shallow part, or Sara swimming laps ten yards away. But the star is undeniably Pippi. She swims toward the camera right before the video fades to black. She's not chopping or leaping or rolling, but successfully swimming, head above water, paws underneath. She's grinning as though she's proud.

I watched that video over and over. The final time I watched it, I stopped seeing Pippi and started noticing Tory. She stood in the background, an ambiguous silhouette against deep green weeds. Even after a year, I couldn't look at her without anger and regret, a combination that caused an empty thudding right in the pit of my stomach.

Sitting in that hotel room, waiting to go home, it suddenly hit me that I had never checked Tory off my mental list of rescued dogs. She had never blossomed. Not really.

21

Puppy Mama

I surveyed the peaceful scene in the front yard. Mason had recently cut the grass. The scent of fresh trimmings infused every breath. The grass spread for a half-acre and stopped at our two-lane country road. One huge evergreen tree stood in our front yard and blocked the entire porch. The evergreen reached seventy feet high and thirty feet wide. It was an enormous, proud tree with perfect proportions, as perfect as the trees at the White House or Rockefeller Center during the holidays. The evergreen had been there long before we arrived, and we treated it with the respect it deserved. At some point, we had even named it Mr. Pine. My mother-in-law, a realtor, had once recommended we cut Mr. Pine down because it shaded half the house. Mason and I had been horrified, as though she'd said we should bulldoze our home or throw our dogs over the fence.

Our front yard was half the size of the back and didn't have a fence, but it was the perfect space for feeding puppies. The Magic 8 ate four times throughout the day in four-hour increments. I had just finished preparing their second meal of the day. In Mr. Pine's shadow, I had placed two large plastic trays. Eight cat-size bowls filled with mush sat on each one. The ground rice and chicken came out of a can, but I poured a blended concoction over it. The creamy liquid consisted of a powder formula mixed with eggs, liquid vitamins, whole milk, and honey.

The scene looked organized and tranquil. I felt a swell of satisfaction, but it only lasted for seconds because I knew as soon as I released the puppies, any tranquility would evaporate. Even so, it didn't bother me that much, not back then. Moments spent with the Magic 8 *were* magic. They brimmed with energy and purpose, and I was addicted.

Mason and I had converted the spare bedroom into a puppy nursery. We cleared out the furniture and covered the hardwood floors with drop cloths and newspapers. A trash can, hamper, clean towels, blankets, paper towels, sponges, wet wipes, and glass cleaner stocked a corner shelf. On the wall, I posted notecards with headshots that cataloged name, gender, weight, and deworming and feeding schedules. We had named the pups after *Sopranos* characters, in order from the biggest to the runt: Junior Soprano, Angie Bonpensiero, Livia Soprano, Jeannie Cusamano, Gloria Trillo, Charmaine Bucco, Adriana La Cerva, and A. J. Soprano.

Taking care of eight three-week-old puppies involved multitasking, organization, and patience, but it also involved a strong stomach. The smell of poop walloped me the second I opened the nursery door. All eight pups slept in a large crate on towels spread over heating pads. They slept in a bundle at the rear corner, mashed together. Several piles of waste littered the newspaper outside the crate. Even at three weeks, they didn't go to the bathroom where they slept.

I gagged once, then again, gained my composure, and walked inside the nursery. The door hinge squeaked. One snoozing fur ball morphed into eight puppies sitting at attention. Their ears had grown into dwarf-size versions of the floppy kind. Their snouts and bodies looked similar, but each wore different patterns. Jeannie, Gloria, and A. J. sported black coats with bright white smudges; Adriana, Angie, and Livia donned primarily golden-beige fur with white circles; Charmaine had a black mask and Junior wore a combination of all the colors, black, white, blond, and dark brown. The same color on different dogs matched so closely it looked as though four paint cans had exploded in Dawn's belly.

Sixteen glistening black eyes stared at me in complete adoration before they stampeded out of the crate. Two stragglers stepped in separate piles of poop and trailed brown smudges. I swept them off the floor, grabbed a wet wipe, and cleaned their paws as I led the troops out front. In just a few short days, I had become their puppy mama.

The Magic 8 waddled down the hallway. Their little paws drummed against the hardwood in a chaotic, unsynchronized rhythm. The two concrete steps off the patio slowed them down. Some paused before trying to maneuver a six-inch drop, but others, like Junior, were too excited to wait and rolled down both steps. When they reached the grass, they charged toward the trays. And that peaceful scene from a few moments ago exploded.

The eight previously adorable puppies turned into fiends who devoured their mush with angry, slurping sounds. They acted as though they hadn't eaten in weeks instead of four short hours. In minutes, they managed to smear the creamy brown concoction onto every body part, including their ears and tail. Some abandoned any remnant of manners and plopped down in their bowls, squishing the food over the trays. Watching them, it was hard to believe that by the time they finished, the only mush remaining would be on their fur. They would clean every inch of those trays.

Our pack, plus Pippi and Tory, were sunbathing on the deck. After the older dogs had walked, eaten, and patrolled the backyard, they gathered on the deck and sunbathed for as long as they could handle the heat. When they had their fill, they would meander into the kitchen, spread their stomachs over the cool kitchen tiles, and sleep until it was time for our afternoon walk. The deck was built on the west side of the house and curved around the back. It had wooden slats for fencing. A small gate with a set of five stairs restricted access to the front yard. I'd carved m3jd, the initials in my tattoo, on the concrete step at the base.

The sun glimmered off Miss Annie's coat. Her hair was turning white and losing its amber tones, but the texture stayed silky. She lifted her head and squinted through the glare. We made eye contact for a brief second. I felt that familiar surge of gratefulness for having her in my life. She plopped her head back down, as though she was drunk off the sun. She would stay outside longer than anybody else, until she panted so hard her tongue grew wide and rose pink. Annie didn't care about the puppies or the mush. Some of her nonchalance had to do with her conviction that she wasn't *really* a dog; but at fifteen she didn't need uncontrollable puppies jumping on her arthritic legs.

It was easy to keep an eye on the Magic 8 while they thrashed in the mush; however, afterward they wandered in eight different directions to do their business. Some stayed close to Mr. Pine, but others roamed to the tree line or near the road. That's when I needed help. For the most part, I was the only one taking care of the puppies. It wasn't that Mason wasn't willing to help, it's that he couldn't. That summer he was out of town five days a week. During the two he spent at home, he didn't have time for much else besides mowing, laundry, and sleep. If Pippi hadn't been living with us that summer, one of those eight puppies could easily have wandered into the woods or onto the road.

Pippi had started herding the puppies from the moment she met them. Whether it was in our living room or yard, she made sure they stayed within her sight. When one wandered, she would nudge them back toward the house, using the gentlest touch, as though she understood they were delicate. If one needed reprimanding, she would growl. In extreme cases, she nipped their ruff. And they would instantly respond. When they all finished their business and gathered close, Pippi didn't stop guarding them. But she did find a shady place for her lookout, because it was a tough business rounding up eight puppies in late June.

Playtime followed eating and bathroom breaks. When the older dogs wrestled in the backyard, it looked graceful and exhilarating, at times frightening. But watching those puppies play was pure entertainment. Junior dominated their mock fighting matches because of his size alone. He simply plowed through anybody who got in his way. Jeannie was the feistiest and Adriana was the loner. Ade scuffled for a few minutes, but when it got too rough she wandered off and chewed on a rubber leaf or a twig. It was during these play sessions that I started seeing their personalities, because even then they possessed unique characteristics. They were becoming individuals. The puppies played until they were exhausted, then fell asleep in their signature cuddle pile. Soon, I'd carry them inside to take their fifth nap of the day. Then, I'd be able to scoop their waste from the yard and clean their nursery.

I'd wanted something to distract me after Joe died, and I got my wish, eight times over. My days were extraordinarily busy, packed with hundreds of tasks associated with being a puppy mama. I didn't stop moving from the time I woke until I hit my pillow. Yet it was all worth it. All my work was paying off because the puppies, even the lethargic ones, were rebounding. After days of structured meals and sleeping in a warm, clean, and safe environment, they were reenergized. Even the runt acted lively. They were all going to survive.

I felt happier than I had for months. The Magic 8 brought an infusion of energy into our house that had been missing. With Joe, we had worked hard, but all our efforts had been focused on dying, not living. With the Magic 8, our work yielded life: hilarious, enchanting puppy life. I felt naturally high, so high I never thought about how fast I was moving. I didn't stop to consider that taking care of fifteen dogs without any help in an already full house might be a bigger challenge than I could handle.

There's a saying among animal welfare groups: "rescue the rescuer." I heard it the first time while visiting the Puget Sound Goat Rescue in Washington. The director, Barbara Jamison, shared a story about piling seventeen baby goats into her Honda Pilot because if she didn't take them home they would have starved to death. "Starvation is a terrible way to die," she said.

At that time, her nonprofit had been new and lacked volunteers and resources, and she'd been overwhelmed for weeks. She told me there was such a thing as doing too much good. But I didn't *realize* that back then; I believed I had karma on my side. I was spreading positive energy and doing good work, so there wasn't a limit to how much I could handle. Melissa Armstrong, the Wonder Woman of Dog Rescue. What could go wrong? But everyone has a limit. Like Barbara said, there's even a limit to doing the right thing. I paid a heavy price for not understanding that.

22

THE WORST THING IMAGINABLE

I shifted into high gear as soon as I walked through our front door. Mason and I had just returned after an evening stroll with Miss Annie and Dessie. The Magic 8 had been living with us for four days and an overwhelming number of chores waited. All fifteen dogs needed to be fed. I had to swap the laundry, sweep the hardwood floors, and deworm the puppies. I got caught up in the swirl of doing twenty things at one time. I scooted into the basement and grabbed a load of warm laundry out of the dryer. Miss Annie loved sleeping in warm clothes. She had, surprisingly, walked two miles and I knew she'd be sore. The heat would help soothe her joints.

Our unfinished basement, which ran the length of the house, had concrete floors, cinder block walls, and exposed pipes on the ceiling. It wasn't the coziest room in the house, and Annie rarely went downstairs. It was the one place she never followed me. She waited on the top step and spun, as though she anticipated the toasty clothes. Pippi and Tory, always curious about Annie, stood on each side, sandwiching her. When I reached the top of the stairs, I could tell she felt crowded. I set the basket down and turned around to pick her up.

I looked away for one second, and in those thirty frames the worst thing imaginable happened. In her shuffling, Tory knocked into Miss

Annie. Annie lost her balance, bounced off the top step, and dropped off the unfinished side, falling eight feet onto the concrete floor. I remember reaching for her and not even coming close to catching her.

Miss Annie never made a sound. Not one cry. Mason said all he heard was my scream. When I picked Annie's body off the concrete, her heart stomped through her rib cage and her neck hung limp. Mason carried her to the front porch.

"Something's wrong. Something's really wrong," he said.

I had the wild idea Dr. Dan would save her, if we got there fast enough. I raced inside for my keys, and by the time I returned it was too late. Mason was hunched over her body.

"She's gone," he said.

But I already knew it. I knew it from the moment I saw her fall. A bigger dog could have survived the fall, but Miss Annie had no chance.

* * *

Earlier that evening Miss Annie had trotted along the asphalt trail, her butt bouncing in rhythm to her steps. Annie walked with a swagger, the kind that came from a lifetime of being loved and protected. Annie's ears swiveled toward the sound of a beaver diving into the creek and a squirrel leaping from limbs. I wouldn't have noticed them if I wasn't paying attention to her.

Another squirrel darted across the greenway less than ten feet away. Miss Annie assumed her hunting pose, body rigid and slanted forward, front paw lifted. The squirrel scurried up an oak and disappeared into the leafy canopy. Annie was fifteen and too old to chase squirrels, but she still loved walking. So did Dessie, who completely ignored the squirrel and trotted next to Mason. She had arthritis in both hips and moved with a prominent limp, so we let her set the pace. Her rear paw scratched against the pavement every other step. The sultry air frizzed the shaggy hair around her ears, making it look as though someone had crimped it with an iron. Besides Joe, Dessie was the only dog Annie cared about.

The fading sun tinted a field in a golden hue. Moths, butterflies, honeybees, and gnats hovered above wildflowers and dandelions. The wild lilac bushes smelled thick, as though the scent stuck to the humidity. An old cottonwood tree, standing at the field's highest point, was shedding its flowers. The small puffballs sprinkled the air like summer's version of snow.

How could Annie die on such an evening? I was so unprepared for the worst thing imaginable. The juxtaposition of her death against the beauty of that night twisted inside me until every detail of that walk ached. Yet, in the aftermath, it was the only memory I thought about. I clutched onto that hour, that one perfect hour, because remembering what happened afterward was unthinkable.

At the very end of the walk, Miss Annie had jumped on my shin, her signal for *pick me up*. She kissed the tip of my nose. I don't remember the very last time Annie and I made eye contact, the last moment we checked on one another. It must have happened on that walk, maybe even on the ride home; but I can't picture it. I do remember that last kiss. I remember the weight of her tiny body and touch of her tongue. I remember her stinky breath and her fur tickling my chin. If only I had known, I never would have let her go.

23

Eighteen Days

The morning was gray. Dessie softly snored from the footstool. Her breathing created a rhythm as familiar as the fan's whirl. Floyd slept near my feet, resting his sturdy weight against my shins. I couldn't physically see Meadow and Sara. They wore the thickest coats and preferred sleeping on cooler spaces, like the hardwood floors or a dog bed. They were quiet sleepers. Sometimes, Meadow fell asleep next to Mason, but she never lasted through the night. Mason spooned me. I pulled his arm closer to my chest because, like my dogs, he anchored me to everything good in the world.

Miss Annie's pink blanket was spread across our bodies. I slid my fingers across the sheets, reaching for Annie so I could pull her toaster-oven-warm body close. My fingers touched the end of the bed and found nothing but cold sheets. All of this happened within seconds. Then with a swift pain, so sharp it took my breath away, I realized the worst thing imaginable had happened. Annie was dead. That moment of not knowing, when I reached for Miss Annie right before I became fully conscious, happened every morning.

* * *

Mason spent the afternoon after Miss Annie died calling our inner circle. Some texted their sympathies, others left messages I never listened to. The sadness in their voices only confirmed what I didn't want to think about, what I couldn't *stop* thinking about. I couldn't form the words *Annie's dead* in my throat. And I sure as hell wasn't putting them on paper. Some part of me believed that if I didn't say it out loud or write it down, it wouldn't be true. In the aftermath, I slept four hours a night, dropped fifteen pounds, and stopped ingesting anything except for green tea and cough drops. I was on the verge of falling into a clinical depression.

Miss Annie disappeared so suddenly I hadn't been able to say goodbye, and that unchangeable truth lingered at the periphery of my mind from dawn until dusk. Joe and I had been square when he died. Our farewell had been proper and meaningful. It included closure. I had so much left to say to Miss Annie that I felt betrayed, and spent days seething with anger. If she couldn't be here, then why had I known her at all? But I *had* known her. And the loss of her eyes following me was a crater-size cavity in my chest.

Just as Joe's shadow always appeared in the woods, so did Annie's in every corner of the house. Sometimes, I heard her tags ringing or tiny paws tapping down the hardwood floors. I glimpsed her ears poking out of the pink blanket and her silky hair shimmering in a square of sunshine. I felt her eyes tracking my movements from room to room. Then I realized it couldn't be true; it would never be true again. The hardest part was figuring out who I was without Miss Annie. When you love someone with so much of your heart, what do you fill that space with when they're gone?

* * *

Joan called three days after Annie died. "How are you feeling?"

"Okay," I answered.

I didn't recognize my voice. I felt separated from it, like it came from someone else's mouth, someone who borrowed my body. Every day felt like that, as though I participated in life but wasn't emotionally attached; it was as if I lived in a snow globe. I replayed the moments leading up to Annie's death in slow motion, but I watched with a sense of otherness. That disconnected feeling stuck around long after the initial shock. I mopped floors, vacuumed, dusted windowsills, folded laundry. I walked and fed the other dogs in our house, but I was disengaged from all of it.

"I'm so sorry," Joan said. Her voice caught on *so*. I knew she held back her tears for my sake.

"Thank you." I was a robot.

"We ordered a catchpole," she said.

"Good."

"You heard that Dawn's back?" she asked.

"I heard," I answered, but I didn't care. I didn't care if Dawn lived on Sycamore Street for the rest of her life. Nothing mattered now that the worst thing imaginable had happened.

"Only she has mange," Joan said. She continued talking about an oral drug the vet said Bernice could mix into her food, but I tuned her out.

* * *

I hated Tory. When I caught a peek of her salt-and-pepper coat or gleaming black eyes, I instantly pictured her bumping Annie. I was the old Melissa; the dramatic Melissa who wanted to throw Tory over our fence. I visualized kicking her out, saw the lush woods swallowing her in its green cocoon.

But I had changed. Annie had changed me. Ironically, the same sense of detachment that separated my emotions from my actions made living with Tory manageable. I physically treated her like the other dogs, but it was all from outside the snow globe. Since dogs are masters at reading body language, it was impossible to hide my feelings from Tory. She knew how I felt and kept her distance.

Mason was the only person who knew about Tory's role in Miss Annie's death. He said that anyone could have bumped into Annie, even one of our dogs. *Tory didn't do it maliciously. She didn't push Annie down the stairs. It was a tragic accident, but it was an accident.* When I listened to Mason, I didn't blame Tory. I didn't blame myself. But when my husband traveled, his voice faded. Tory killed Annie. I saw it happen. And it was my fault.

I scrubbed out Annie's dog bowl, a purple dish decorated with white hearts that was as small as a saucer. I used a bristled sponge to wipe the crumbs of her dog food out of the crevices. I picked up her squeaky soccer balls, four in all. I wrapped up her nylon leash, soft from wear and thin enough to slide through my fingers. I folded her sweaters. She owned five, four of which she had tried on once. The one she liked was a thick brown knit with colored flowers sewn onto the collar. She only wore it in the winter, when the temperature sunk below freezing. She had twirled whenever I pulled it out. I packed all of it in a plastic storage box. How could fifteen years fit into a box big enough to store in a closet? How had such a big personality crammed itself into such a small dog? When Joe died, I doubted our family would ever be the same. Now, I knew it wouldn't. And I didn't know if I wanted it to be the same, because the pain was so severe I never wanted to feel this sort of loss again. Losing Annie made me love everyone less.

Miss Annie's dog tag and her pink blanket were the only things I didn't pack away. I hung her tag from my neck with a lengthy piece of leather. It was shaped like a heart. The pink glossy coating had smudged away where the tag rubbed against her harness, but her name was still perfectly legible. The pink blanket was even older. Miss Annie and I had found it in a thrift store the first year I dated Mason. The color palette in the knitted pattern ranged from pale to rose-colored pink. It wasn't wide but long, designed for a twin mattress. The blanket wore some small holes and frayed ends after years of use, but it was just as heavy as the day we found it. Just like when Annie was alive, I slept with it every night.

* * *

I stared at a poem someone sent me. It's called "Rainbow Bridge." The author is unknown. "When an animal dies that has been especially close to someone here, that pet goes to Rainbow Bridge," says the website (rainbowsbridge.com) dedicated to the poem. It continues, "and when you and your special friend finally meet, you cling together in joyous reunion, never to be parted again." It's a sentimental poem, at times downright sappy, but it suggests an afterlife. I read it multiple times, thinking if I read it enough maybe I'd believe it. I've never wanted to believe in God and heaven as much as I did after Miss Annie's accident. I told myself I'd see Annie again if I believed, but my intuition countered every time. Rainbow Bridge was just a fantasy. I crumpled up the poem and threw it in the trash can.

* * *

I smelled the stench seconds before I saw the wreckage. When I opened the door, I gaped at the nursery, unable to comprehend how such small animals had produced such mass destruction in such a short time. The nursery smelled like a sewer and looked as if someone had plowed through it with a lawn mower. The puppies had knocked over a waste can and torn up dirty paper towels, plus had pulled a new roll off the shelf. They had shredded all of it into a confetti that floated in the fan's breeze like motes. Three extra-large books that had been pushed to the farthest corner were demolished. The only one left intact was on the bottom. They had managed to gnaw through the binder of a two-thousand-page dictionary and completely gut a phone book. At least ten piles of poop dotted the floor, some flattened into pancakes and others spread like soft butter. Somehow, they had smeared it on the walls. I closed my eyes and counted backward from ten.

The puppies were sound asleep in their crate, a mound of rising and falling fur. They'd shifted when I'd opened the door but didn't wake up. If the mess in the nursery was any indication, the puppies were exhausted because they'd expended all their energy making it. I had accidentally forgotten to latch their crate before I left home. I'd been gone for two short hours and had returned to an apocalypse. I'd been wrong all along. Puppies weren't cute. They were needy blobs with tails that looked like they belonged on rats.

I sank to the floor. I felt so overwhelmed that I wanted to crawl into bed and forget about all of it. I couldn't even take care of one six-pound dog; how could I take care of fifteen? *If I didn't have fifteen fucking dogs in the house, eight of whom were one-month-old puppies, then Annie would still be alive. She was dead because of me.*

At some point during my emotional beatdown, Adriana La Cerva crawled onto my lap. I felt her body heat before I saw the little blond dog cuddled on my baggy jeans. She rested her snout against my big toe, with chipped red polish and calluses that needed sanding. She didn't care and even licked it once or twice. Stroking her fur, my panic slowed to a trickle. I thought about the reality of my situation. Being depressed wasn't an option. I had to keep going because Ade needed me. They all needed me. The mess wouldn't disappear, no matter how much I beat myself up. The stench would simply leak into the rest of the house. After a few more minutes, I put on a pair of rubber gloves, grabbed a trash bag, and started cleaning.

* * *

Almost three weeks after Annie died, I stood on the patio with a bucket in one hand and a pooper-scooper in the other. Every time one of the puppies did their business, I shoveled up the turd, now thankfully worm-free. I'd throw the waste in the woods later. The July sun blared down like florescent bulbs in a tanning booth. I squinted it away. The heat was oppressive.

It was so hot that even Pippi napped under Mr. Pine's branches. She only moved when one of the puppies wandered too far away. Junior was still squatting over his empty food bowl, spreading all four legs wide for optimum balance. There wasn't any food left, but he wasn't convinced.

He outweighed the runt by three pounds. The puppies didn't seem to mind the heat, at least not right after breakfast. But I had learned that the roasting temperatures would tire them faster. It couldn't happen fast enough.

The loner, Adriana, entertained herself by gnawing on the outer bark of a magnolia tree. She suddenly cocked her head, as though she saw something exciting. She had spotted a mammoth sunflower I'd thrown into the compost pile. The flower's head was double the size of her own, the stalk longer than her body. It took her a few moments to figure out how to pick it up, but once she did, she ran circles around her littermates with it clutched in her mouth. Her body language, jaunty step, and high tail and snout communicated her pride. The flower attracted every one of the puppies. They scrambled after her in mad pursuit. Adriana ran so hard, she flipped ass over teakettle a few times, but she bounced right back up and kept running. I laughed—a spontaneous, out-loud, belly-rumbling one. The sound surprised me. I'd forgotten how good it felt.

* * *

The mattress stretched around me. The clock read 2:30 a.m. I'd been staring at it for hours. Annie had died eighteen days ago, but sleeping without her was becoming harder, not easier. I forced myself to think happy thoughts, like how earlier that day Adriana had found a sunflower. Her joy over that new toy was more proof that happiness can be found in simplicity. Laughing had felt like a replay of the old me, the person I was before the worst thing imaginable happened. I wanted to be that person again, but I didn't know if I could. I didn't know if I was brave enough to love that much again.

I tiptoed into the nursery, pulled Adriana from the pile, and carried her into our bedroom. She rested in my hands like a rag doll, as though she completely trusted me. Back in high school, my friends and I had played a game of trust, in which we fell backward into a friend's arms. If we tensed, it meant we didn't trust our partner. But if we fell backward without stiffening one muscle, we did. Although I didn't understand it back then, our game had been about body language. And if I read Ade's correctly, she trusted me, and her conviction soothed all my bruised emotions.

About seven hours later, I edged toward consciousness. It was the first time I'd slept for any solid length of time in weeks. Like every morning, I reached for Miss Annie. But instead of finding cold sheets, I found a warm body. Adriana was sleeping in Annie's spot. I immediately knew she wasn't Miss Annie. Her fur wasn't as silky; her body wasn't as fragile. I felt a pang of disappointment followed immediately by a sense of wonder that Adriana had burrowed under the quilt sometime during the night. I gently slid Adriana to my chest and inhaled her puppy breath.

Eighteen days after Annie died, I wrote a blog post and told the whole world about the worst thing imaginable. It was the first time I'd told anyone.

24

WHY DAWN HATED HUMANS

Dawn's runt, A. J., bounded after a monarch butterfly that was drinking from milkweed growing inside the tree line. He didn't have a chance of catching the colorful orange insect, but he didn't know that and chased it with determination. It seemed like the butterfly flirted with him, swooping above his ears as it fluttered from one plant to the next. Branches slung shadows across the yard. In places, they camouflaged the puppy's black silhouette; at times, they completely obscured him. At one point, A. J. spun at such an angle that the blaze of white fur across his chest was the only part visible. His looked like his mother's miniature. He looked like Dawn.

Watching A. J., it struck me that I wanted to find out if Jimmy's story was true: if the police shot those dogs. I hadn't thought much about Dawn since Annie's accident. And I never thought about trying to catch her anymore. When Annie died, I stopped caring. Sometimes, I even wondered if I had the emotional strength to continue fostering dogs for Free Love. But suddenly, the need to discover what happened in that field was all that mattered.

The idea that our local law enforcement could sanction something so brutal and dangerous seemed outrageous. Mason still said opening fire in city limits wasn't legal. I wanted to believe men with his integrity ran our police force, but I had serious doubts—doubts based in experience, not rumor. I'd faced Tennessee's outdated laws the first time over a decade ago, and its memory resurfaced whenever I thought about Jimmy's story.

* * *

A year after Mason and I had moved to West End Avenue in Nashville, our buddy Larry Penning called. Larry lived with a semipro racecar driver whom he'd known since childhood.

"His dog looks bad," Larry said. "I think there's something wrong with her."

"What can we do?" I asked.

"The key is under the gnome on the front porch," he said. "She's in the backyard. Will you take a look at her?"

They lived in Smyrna, twenty minutes southwest of our apartment. Their place was a mansion that sat in a row of identical-looking mansions built in a community named something like Pine Willow or Pine Heights. I tipped the generic plaster gnome, red hat and blue vest, found the key, and unlocked the front door.

On the ride, I had tried conjuring a sick dog, the kind who forced Larry to ask for a favor. Larry wasn't a close friend, so his call surprised me, but it also meant that the dog must have been in trouble. In retrospect, no imagery could have prepared me for my first encounter with an abused animal. Sure, I watched the same newscasts and horror flicks as everybody else, but seeing cruelty in real life is much different. Above all, there's no separation, no screen, no chance for disbelief whatsoever.

The temperature teetered at freezing. A heavy mist fell from the slate sky. I glanced once at the dog, and then closed my eyes, tilted my face upward, and focused on the rain coating my cheeks. I inhaled so intently I smelled the hydrogen atoms in the thick, wet air. I was trying to stretch out each second, trying to find an "off" button that didn't exist, not in that backyard.

But I couldn't look away any longer. The Doberman, maybe six months old, hunkered down in the corner of a twelve-foot privacy fence. The fence hid her emaciated body from any neighbor's view. If she could talk, she could have called for help, but without words and behind that fence, she was invisible.

I knew she was a dog, yet in that moment she didn't look like one. She looked more like a dragon, and right then I named her Puff, after the animal in the children's song. Her coloring was gray, like the mist falling around her, and the rain painted her coat in the same metallic sheen as a dragon's. Her ribs, spine, and hipbones jutted through her skin like dragon-size scales, each bone so vividly drawn that each could be counted. Her ears were geometrically opposed: one stood straight up, the other pointed straight out. A substance thicker than urine dripped from her vagina.

Either she wasn't a fighter or someone had beaten the fight out of her, because she let us approach without showing an ounce of aggression. As I stood and stared at that pathetic animal, I digested the reality of a starving dog living with a rich man, a man who owned a mansion. The incongruity of it infuriated me.

Mason lifted Puff into his arms and retraced our steps through the house and to the car. I locked the front door behind us and replaced the key under the gnome. It was as simple as that. We never discussed taking her or not. We simply reacted. Who would do anything differently?

In retrospect, that's when my idealism turned into action. I'd been an idealist since childhood and lived with a need to help others, but I never knew how to direct my anguish. Before Puff, that uncertainty caused a lot of guilt; afterward, I knew I'd spend the rest of my life saving dogs.

We drove straight to the VCA Murphy Road Animal Hospital. Dr. Lewis said Puff suffered from starvation and had a urinary tract infection. Some sort of blow had permanently damaged the cartilage in her ear. Dr. Lewis, thirtyish and tall, with long blond hair, cried when she fed Puff a handful of food, gave her an antibiotic shot, and wrapped a diaper around her back end. She advised feeding Puff small quantities every couple of hours. A week of medicine would cure her infection. Dr.

Lewis didn't charge us for the visit or the medication. I lost track of her after we moved to Robertson County, but I'll never forget her empathy on that day.

Our next stop was the Davidson County Animal Control office. Mason set Puff on the tile floor, right in front of the officer. The dog slowly slid to her stomach, four knobby legs spreading in different directions. With a diaper around her behind and eyes clouded with medication, she looked even more pitiful than she had in the backyard. Mason tried explaining the situation to the animal control officer, but he skipped over the most important part. I interrupted him.

"He's rich. And he did this." My voice trembled with anger. The owner's wealth exacerbated his crime a thousand percent, and even now my feelings haven't changed. I feel empathy for people who love dogs but underestimate the high cost of feeding and vetting them. I understand how the love of an animal overcomes fiscal sense, and how fundamentally unfair it is that having healthy animals is becoming a middle-class privilege. But this man was different. He paid thousands of dollars for a purebred Doberman, yet he treated her without an ounce of empathy. He had the resources to give Puff a healthy life; instead, he starved her behind a twelve-foot privacy fence. In my eyes, that's torture.

The officer touched Puff's ear and sighed. The officer had short dark hair and a stocky build. She wore a green uniform with creases ironed down the legs. The soles on her black sneakers were thick, thick enough to absorb the shock of hearing stories about abused dogs all day. She jotted down notes in a lined notepad and chewed on her eraser for what seemed like a long time.

"How did you get into his house again?" she asked.

"His roommate told me the key was under the gnome," I said. "We let ourselves in."

"Let me get this straight. The owner didn't give you permission to enter his house?"

I shook my head.

"In the state of Tennessee, dogs are considered property. Basically, the way the law reads you broke into this man's house without his permission and stole his property," she said.

"We did something wrong?" Mason asked. He sounded incredulous.

"According to the law, you did," she said.

"There's nothing we can do to him?" I couldn't comprehend the unfairness of it. I'd been convinced the owner would spend a night behind bars, have his mug shot published in the paper, and *at least* get a ticket. How could there not be consequences? A clock signaled the changing hour. Papers shuffled. A draft hit my nape. The officer's badge glimmered with authority. It all clicked together. We had committed a crime by rescuing Puff, and the man who starved and beat her had done nothing wrong. It was legalized cruelty.

The silence that filled her cubicle was weightless. The officer cleared her throat. "Look, as far as I'm concerned this dog is dead. It got out of the fence and got hit by a car. Do you understand what I'm telling you?"

I didn't realize the officer was doing us a favor back then. I left her cubicle without a thank you or a goodbye. Now, I understand she was as generous as Dr. Lewis. When Puff recovered, we found her a home far away from Smyrna.

* * *

Thirteen years later, I drove to the Springfield Police Station thinking about the similarities between Puff and Dawn. Granted, a rich racecar driver starving a dog was different than cops shooting a pack—yet both were equally cruel. In my reasoning, both instances sprung from the conviction that animals were as expendable as property.

On the other hand, I couldn't define my community based on laws alone. I thought about Bernice and Jimmy using their meager incomes on food for animals they didn't even own. I thought about the Farnival reader Beth, who'd paid for Buddy's medical costs, and Joan, who saved hundreds of homeless animals through her nonprofit. In that ambivalent space where

I both liked and disliked my southern home, I admitted there was a chance the police were the good guys after all. Maybe they didn't do it.

Now, I realize I held on to that possibility because I wanted to believe it. After years of seeing dogs like Puff, Floyd, Sara, and Meadow, dogs like Dawn, I'd gotten tougher, harder. I'd grown a crust around my heart. Yet I couldn't crush hope, the essential ingredient in every activist. It's like hope is wired into our DNA. I wanted to be wrong. I wanted it so much that, up to the second I approached the glass door, I considered going home. I considered pretending it didn't happen. After all, I was still emotionally vulnerable, still grieving for Miss Annie. I was just starting to feel okay again. What if it was true? Who would care anyway? And what could I even do if it was true?

I opened the glass door of the police station with an anguish that made walking forward seem as slow as wading through water. During my fifteen years in sports broadcasting, I've interviewed scores of professional athletes, mostly competitive men. I've experienced the unease associated with asking tough questions. But I felt like a rookie standing in that police station. I approached the receptionist.

"I need to talk to someone about police officers shooting a pack of stray dogs behind Sycamore Street in the summer of 2013," I blurted out.

The office assistant's eyes widened. She spun around and whispered to another clerk sharing her cinder block cubicle. A hushed debate ensued before she asked me to sit in the waiting room, which was a hallway painted lead gray with a few metal folding chairs lined against the walls. Heavy doors on each side locked with a resounding thud when they closed. Slate tiles covered the floor. Occasionally, officers walked past wearing the same thick soles as the officer at Davidson County Animal Control all those years ago. Their badges glimmered with the same authority. The clock had the same round face and same ticking hands.

Finally, a middle-aged woman emerged and introduced herself as the police chief's assistant, Mrs. Tami Evans. I repeated Jimmy's story and explained that I wasn't trying to make trouble. And I wasn't. At that point, I wasn't thinking about anything beyond getting confirmation or denial. Mrs. Evans paused. The way she summed me up from behind her bangs, the way she couldn't meet my eye, the way she carefully printed my name and phone number in her notepad told me all I needed to know. She acted too meticulously for a rumor. They had done it. If Jimmy's calculations were right, Dawn had been around six months old when the shooting occurred, the equivalent of a three-year-old child.

Mrs. Evans led me to a small conference room furnished with sheer curtains, faux-leather seats, and a polished wood table—a completely different setting than the rigid waiting room with its metal and concrete. After a short wait, I spoke with Lieutenant Maynar, an officer with gray hair and ruddy cheeks. The lieutenant was polite, often calling me "ma'am." He confirmed the incident with a southern accent that in any other circumstance would have been charming. Instead, his twang sounded dated and stereotypical.

He said that particular pack was "vicious" and "harming property," so officers "set up a situation" where they could "destroy" the "feral dogs." He made it very clear this sort of "extermination" is legal in Robertson County. The lieutenant's tone softened at some point. Maybe he realized I wasn't there for an argument. He said the Springfield Police Department had ordered a net gun, which was a more humane way to capture feral dogs. He even offered to help us catch Dawn if we hadn't trapped her by the time their net gun arrived. I thanked him for his honesty before I left.

I sat in my car outside the police station and switched the air-conditioning to full blast. Outside my window, a frayed American flag hung lifeless in the humid air. Water stained the red, white, and blue fabric. I had walked into the police station wondering what I'd do if I confirmed Jimmy's story and walked out asking myself the same questions: *Why did I come here? Why do I need to know what happened?* It would have been easier to ignore the whole situation.

That evening, I watched the puppies finish their dinner. A. J. meandered toward the milkweed. He was looking for the same monarch butterfly he had played with that morning. It had moved on, but he remembered; just like his mother remembered that day in the field.

The shooting explained Dawn's inordinate fear and why she wouldn't let anyone touch her. I thought about the lieutenant's stoic face when he said "destroy." How did he remain impassive? Anger swelled inside me. I'd been angry a lot since Annie died, but this anger was different. It was more like outrage, the same kind I had felt about Puff. Tennessee's laws may legalize cruelty, but that didn't mean I had to accept it. On that evening, I silently reaffirmed my promise to Bernice. I would catch Dawn. I would make sure she never got shot in a field. It was the only way to respond to what happened behind that halfway house.

25

TORY AND PATTY HARVEY

Charles Harvey waited for us at the end of his driveway. He wore a gray beard and black leather newsboy hat. I'd never met him before, but Joan had interviewed him extensively; she was serious about maintaining a rigorous vetting process for all potential adopters. If they got through her personal questions, such as income and family history, then Free Love conducted a home visit. If families didn't want us coming to their house for any reason, they were immediately struck off. Joan did everything in her power to find the right homes for Free Love's dogs.

Joan pulled her minivan into the Harveys' driveway. Their house looked small but tidy. Tory stuck her head between the bucket seats, her tail swishing back and forth. She was excited about this new adventure, unaware that if this home visit went well, she would remain with the Harveys.

It took eighteen days for me to admit that Annie died, but months for me to confess Tory's part in it. I kept that information as close as a dirty secret because admitting Tory's guilt was equivalent to me admitting my complicity. I would finally fess up in a room full of strangers. My friend Charlotte and I signed up for a creative writing workshop in downtown Nashville. The instructor provided several writing prompts, sentences or phrases that inspire ideas. I chose one that started, "I never told anyone this, but . . ." The instructor gave us twenty minutes, and I wrote until the last second. When she asked for volunteers to read their work, I stood up in front of twenty people and read, "I never told anyone this, but Tory killed Annie, and so did I."

I often found home visits the most emotional part of the fostering process. It was one of the many instances when I felt the impossible but urgent desire to clearly communicate with dogs. For them, it must have felt like another abandonment. Mason and I were the only stability many of those dogs had ever known, and they all reacted when we left them behind—some more dramatically than others. In one case, Silvio Dante had howled at the top of his hound-dog lungs, so loudly that I'd had to drown him out with my car radio as I drove away. When I said goodbye to Rosalie Aprile and shut the front door behind me, she'd lunged against it so hard that the wood sounded like it might've cracked. Even worse were the dogs who didn't act out but still made their fear clear. Their hopeful eyes would zero in on our retreating backs, as though any second we might change our minds, and that quiet hope was somehow louder than any cry.

Charles's wife, Patty, met us at the door. She was in her late fifties with shoulder-length graying hair. She held a tissue to swollen, weepy eyes, and sniffled frequently. I thought she had allergies until I entered their living room. By the look of the polished tabletop and vacuumed carpets, their home had recently been cleaned. In the center of all that cleanliness, Patty had set up a memorial on a coffee table: an 8 x 10 graduation picture of a young man with feathered hair sat at the center. I guessed it had been taken thirty years earlier. A few snapshots in smaller frames showed an older version of their son. Condolence cards buttressed each side of the table. The phrases "losing a son" and "the loss of a child" were written in bold, graceful script. Candles cast a flickering glow across the pictures' glass surfaces.

Patty was grieving for her son, just like I was grieving for Annie, but she still lived in her snow globe. I didn't need her to tell me that her son's death had been tragic; that one moment he was there and the next he wasn't. She didn't need to explain his death was the worst thing imaginable because I could see it in her bloodshot eyes.

I unhooked Tory's leash. Potential family members were normally the last stop on a dog's initial investigation. The bold ones often sniffed the perimeter, inhaling hundreds of clues about their new environment. The shy ones hid behind my legs, sticking their noses into the familiar scent of my jeans. Tory didn't do, either. It was as though she zeroed in on Patty's need and walked straight toward her. Standing on her back paws, she propped her front legs across Patty's lap and leaned forward. It looked like a canine version of a hug. Patty buried her face in her fur and made a noise that sounded like a quiet moan, as though she was releasing something. I knew that moan. I'd made the same sound on the day I met Miss Annie. Annie had once healed me, and Tory was going to do the same thing for Patty.

When I left, Tory didn't care. She didn't pull or whimper. She didn't even watch me. Tory was crawled up on the carpeted floor next to an armchair, while Patty ran her fingertips through her salt-and-pepper ruff. Patty already loved her in a way I never could.

26

The Best Home for Adriana

Mason and I were lying in bed, probably watching *NCIS* or a show about building bridges on the Discovery Channel. Mason always operated the remote, just like he always drove. The pink blanket was sprawled across our legs. Annie had been gone for a month, but I still needed the blanket's weight at night.

"I talked to Joan today," Mason said.

Meadow rested on the other side of Mason with her head draped across his shoulder. She'd stay next to him until she got too hot, then move to the floor. She doted on him.

"She asked me if you were talking about keeping one of the puppies," he continued.

"Not a chance." I was downright offended.

Miss Annie had only been gone for four weeks. How could Joan possibly think I was ready for another dog? Although with my proclivity toward puppies, I guess I understood why she'd asked. Besides, Joan didn't know I'd changed. Everything had changed. My heart didn't have the space to love another animal because it was too crushed from losing the last. I was too afraid of getting hurt again.

"We've always said it isn't about replacing one dog with another," Mason added. "Those puppies were born on the street. I can't think of anyone who needs a home more right now."

"Not a chance," I snapped. "And you can quit your sales pitch. I know exactly where those puppies were born."

Mason persisted. "Adriana's the one you'd adopt."

"I'm not adopting any."

"But you are sweet on her. And she'd get to keep her name." Mason knew Adriana La Cerva ranked among my five favorite characters on *The Sopranos*. He also knew that when I said "Ade," the little white puppy responded, like she already recognized it as hers.

"Mason, please . . ."

Meadow jumped off the bed, as though she sensed the tension. I pulled the pink blanket up to my neck. Its weight pushed against my chest.

* * *

Laurie Fulsome walked up our gravel driveway with her baby tucked under her arm in the same careless, confident way an athlete carries a ball. During those initial seconds, I summed her up as self-assured and athletic, both positive traits for anyone adopting a dog. Laurie had contacted Joan about adopting both Pippi and a puppy. I pictured Jeannie gnawing on Pippi's enormous ear, A. J. burrowing into her belly for an afternoon nap, and Charmaine yanking on her tail. I remembered those first few weeks and how Pippi had helped herd and train them. The puppies loved Pippi, and I loved the thought of Pippi being with any of them. I *wanted* things to work with Laurie, more than I normally did with a potential adopter.

Several potential adopters were scheduled to stop by our house that afternoon. Most wanted to meet the puppies. The Magic 8 had turned six weeks old in the middle of July. Joan wouldn't allow them to leave Free Love's care until they were two months, but the initial introductions were underway. Joan sat in the shadiest section of our deck, paperwork piled on her lap. When we had first started volunteering, Joan had counseled us to make decisions about families with a "put the dog first" attitude. She'd recommended that we always ask ourselves, *Is this the best home for the dog?* I'd repeated her advice before every meet and greet.

Mason had a rare summer weekend at home. He leaned against the railing, looking completely at ease, as though he hosted meet and greets on a daily basis. As relaxed as he looked, I knew he was logging details of Laurie's visit from under the brim of his baseball cap, details I wouldn't notice without him. These brief encounters with potential adopters required making life-changing decisions in a short amount of time. An extra set of discerning eyes always helped.

Our house was busier during that July than the past six months combined. Besides potential adopters, friends and acquaintances called and asked if they could stop by to see the puppies. Another volunteer for Free Love had brought her sons over, so they could "help" with the Magic 8. Those boys had loved hosing down the pups' bowls, mainly because they ended up soaking each other; but they did help scoop poop. Another friend had driven forty-five minutes up Interstate 24 so he could mix their mush. The UPS man had stopped for a full five minutes and cuddled Jeannie in the crook of his neck before volunteering to carry our heavy boxes of dog food to the basement. Everybody loved the puppies. We'd have no trouble finding them homes, good homes.

Mason offered Laurie a chair, but she declined, sat on the deck, and plopped her baby down in front of her. Pippi immediately, if slowly, approached the infant. I'd seen Pippi around children but never babies, so I was as curious as everybody about how she'd act. Gingerly, she sniffed the child's chubby fingers, nudged the folds of skin behind her knees, and moved to her pea-size toes. The baby's diaper drew her attention for a steady minute. Just like she did with the puppies, Pippi treated the baby with the gentlest touch. At one point, the baby screeched, and Pippi jumped. We all laughed. Pippi tilted her head, probably wondering what caused our outburst. Her shyness was one of the reasons no one had adopted her yet. In the end, Laurie wouldn't adopt her for the same reason. Pippi's interest with the Fulsome family would stop at the baby.

Jackie Fricke, another potential adopter, pulled up minutes after Laurie. Jackie, thirty years old and single, had a steady job, a fenced yard, and an older dog named Gino. She had brought Gino with her because she wanted to see how he got along with Junior. Between her wedge sandals and extra-long leash, Jackie didn't have an ounce of control over her eighty-pound mutt. Gino was fascinated with the multitude of new smells and yanked his teetering master back and forth across the gravel driveway.

Mason rolled his eyes when he saw Jackie's shoes. He often said one of the reasons he fell in love with me was because I never wore anything as impractical as heels. I eventually confessed that I didn't wear heels because I couldn't. When I tried, I was so off-balance it seemed as dangerous as driving drunk. If I hadn't quit trying, I would've hurt somebody by now. Always a gentleman, Mason stepped outside the gate to help Jackie. The day was going perfectly so far. Adopters were showing up on time. I liked Laurie and was willing to remain open about Jackie, even with the long leash and heels.

"Do you know which puppy you're thinking about adopting?" I asked Laurie.

I needed to go inside for Junior and thought I'd grab the one Laurie wanted to meet. The puppies were snoozing on Joe's old dog bed in the living room. All eight of them only took up a quarter of the oblong pillow. I didn't have to worry about them roaming when they slept because they stayed so close it seemed as though they were tethered together.

"I'm really in love with that white one I saw on your blog a few days ago," Laurie said. "I think her name is Adriana."

I heard what she said, but it took me a second to understand it. I had to replay her words more than once. Once it settled, the panic set in. Adriana. She was talking about Adriana. I knew the photo well. Adriana is sitting in the yard, but the grass is out of focus, a green cloud framing her tiny silhouette. Folds of skin rib her arms. She's propped up on her front paws, and her gaze falls to the left of the camera. Her eyes glimmer with clarity, yet they look as black as a moonless sky. My breath had caught in the back of my throat when I first saw the image, but I didn't think my reaction signified anything besides an acknowledgment of her cuteness. I never thought it meant I had feelings about her.

Overcome with unexplainable turmoil, I excused myself and hurried inside. Without considering my actions or asking myself why, I scooped up Adriana, raced down the hallway, plunked her in their crate, and latched the door. I closed the nursery door and reminded myself to breathe. I liked Laurie, didn't I? Was there an inner alarm telling me she wasn't the right person? Was this one of those moments when I needed to listen to my intuition? The very few bits of logic left in my racing mind all said that my actions didn't have anything to do with Laurie. They had everything to do with Adriana.

Forcing myself to move slower and calm down, I gathered Junior and Angie from the pile in the living room and walked outside. For a stranger who knew the litter through pictures alone, the only visible difference between Adriana and Angie was that the latter had dark brown splotches across her rib cage. My heart pounded as fast as a heavy metal riff. *What was I doing?*

"Here's Adriana. The one you were asking about."

"I love her spots," Laurie said. "You couldn't see them in the picture."

"No. You couldn't," I answered.

My heart rate slowed after five minutes. Joan was holding court, explaining our adoption polices to both candidates while simultaneously trying to sum up their characters. After ten minutes, I was confident my little subterfuge would go unnoticed. In fact, the introductions were going so well that I let down my guard and watched the puppies wrestle (or at least try to wrestle) with Gino and Pippi. At six weeks, they were still clumsy, but they were gaining confidence daily. I told myself I'd figure out my feelings later. Maybe, I'd learn to like Laurie so much by the time the pups were ready to leave that I'd change my mind. But not now. Because now, when I thought about someone else holding Adriana, someone else feeding or training her, I felt sick.

As though the universe conspired against me, things suddenly got more complicated because Laurie asked if she could go inside to breast-feed her baby. That meant she'd be thirty feet away from Adriana. I didn't want Laurie any closer to her than she already was, but I couldn't say *no* to a nursing mother. With great anxiety, I showed Laurie into the living room and she situated herself on our couch. The puppies, minus three, slept a few feet away from her.

My heart was beating so loudly it took me a few minutes to hear Adriana's cries, but once I did I couldn't hear anything else. Who could blame her? I had ripped Adriana away from a warm mound of slumbering bliss and locked her alone in the nursery. Tiny whimpers sailed through the hallway and into our living room, so clearly it was as though a speaker hung over our heads. Laurie looked at me with a puzzled expression. I responded with a shrug, hoping Ade would stop before I had to lie. But she didn't. Instead, her whines only got louder, until they were so shrill they were impossible to ignore. Each piercing cry was evidence of my ruse.

"One of the pups doesn't feel well," I said. Sitting on that couch and lying through my teeth, I rationalized my anxiety about Laurie like this: she was raising a baby. She wouldn't have the time or energy for a puppy.

Mason walked into the living room. "Who is screaming?"

"Angie doesn't feel good," I said.

"Angie is out—," he started, but I cut him off with a single look. A moment passed between us, an understanding that only happens between people who intimately know each other's body language and who can't lie to each other with words. Mason had realized long before I had that I'd fallen in love with Adriana.

"Huh," he said, a smile hovering at the corners of his mouth. "She seemed fine a few minutes ago."

"She must have gotten a hold of something," I responded, as airily as I could.

"Must have," he said.

* * *

Later that week, I took Adriana and three other dogs on our four-mile morning walk. It was the first time I'd included any of the Magic 8 in our morning ritual. Adriana weighed seven pounds. I didn't expect her to walk the whole four miles, so I strapped Miss Annie's old papoose over my shoulders in preparation for carrying her at least half the distance. I still hadn't confronted my feelings about that puppy. Every time I tried sorting out my emotions, I felt like I was betraying Miss Annie. I knew it wasn't logical. I knew I could never replace her. Never. But, could I love another dog like that?

At first, I let Ade get acquainted with the leash by dragging it behind her. For short spurts, she held the rope in her tiny maw, acting as though she knew she'd gain speed without the heavy string dragging behind her. A few times she lagged to sniff a nut or swat a cicada. Then, she'd realize how much distance had grown between us and lunge toward us, back paws kicking up pebbles. If we passed pedestrians, I picked her up out of respect for other walkers. Each time I held her off the ground, she squirmed, as if she was a restless child. She made it very clear she didn't want to be held. She wanted to walk with her pack.

Adriana galloped across the two-mile marker with the same gusto she'd started the hike. She was a born walker. If I kept going, she wouldn't stop. I had made up all kinds of excuses about why we shouldn't adopt Adriana: she didn't need us; she was already a great puppy; she was adorable; Free Love would find her a home in a week. All these perfectly valid reasons ran through my mind, but dread clumped inside me whenever I thought about life without her.

I took control of her leash for the last mile. She didn't seem to notice, or if she did, she didn't care. She chugged along, wearing the bewitched smile of a wolf satisfying her instinctual need to migrate. I unbuckled Annie's papoose when we got back to the car. I hadn't used it once.

Adriana followed Meadow into the car. Meadow sat on her hind legs on the passenger seat, and Adriana nestled against the bigger dog's stomach. Meadow rode sitting upright with her head out the window for the entire twenty-minute ride, as though she didn't want to lie down and squash the sleeping puppy. After Annie died, grief took up so much room in my heart that nothing else fit. I thought my heart would stay that way. I wanted it to stay that way. Didn't I? But seeing Adriana cuddled against Meadow answered Joan's question, *Is this the right home for Ade?* It's hard for humans to lie with body language and it's impossible for dogs. Adriana's body was saying she was right where she needed to be. I called Mason and said Adriana wanted to keep her name.

* * *

Joan and I sat on Bernice's porch. I had brought Adriana and Livia over to visit Bernice. They were almost two months old, and the last of the Magic 8 staying at our house. Joan had split the other six into different foster homes. She'd brought Bernice a new quilt from Goodwill and a bag of Kibbles 'n Bits. Mama didn't take any time to stake her claim on the new blanket. She had waddled up the road with Blackberry following as soon as we showed up, as though she smelled the food in Joan's trunk. Just like before, Mama and Blackberry didn't care about the puppies, but the rest of us sat there enchanted while they chased dandelion fluff.

Dawn showed up when we were giggling over Livia growling at a particularly tough weed. In the days following Annie's death, when I was still in the snow globe, Free Love had decided to suspend our efforts to catch Dawn until her mange healed. The vet had prescribed an oral antibiotic that Bernice was slipping in Dawn's food every morning. She had another week of treatment, but her neck looked healthy from twenty yards away. With Dawn being there, it felt like the right moment to talk about my feelings for Adriana.

"If it's okay with everybody here," I said, nodding to Dawn, "I'd like to adopt Adriana."

Within seconds, Bernice answered, "Well, it's about time. I've been wondering how long you'd hold out. Held out longer than I guessed."

"Well, she's found the best home," Joan said when she could finally talk. She was holding back tears. As tough as Joan acted when it came to her nonprofit, she was deeply sentimental about people and animals she cared about.

I turned to Dawn. "Is that okay with you?"

Dawn lay down on the next-door neighbor's driveway and watched her puppies play.

27

Adriana, Two-Time Foster-Failure

Mason and I spent a week vacationing on the West Coast the month after we adopted Adriana. When we had originally planned the trip, Miss Annie was supposed to travel with us. After the worst thing imaginable, I thought about canceling the whole vacation, but Mason talked me into bringing Adriana. "Why not?" he said. "We already have the perfect-size travel bag for her, and we paid the pet fee." So, at two months old, Adriana La Cerva flew with us to Oregon and road tripped from Astoria to the Jedediah Smith Redwoods State Park near Crescent City, California.

Mason and I had been traveling sections of Route 101 between Seattle and San Francisco once a year for the past fifteen years. We had fallen in love with the Northwest coastline on our first date: a six-week road trip from Denver, Colorado, to Seattle, Washington, and then finally San Francisco. On that extended, crazy, exhilarating date, we had opened up about our growing feelings for each other as we sat in front of a bonfire in Crescent City. In order to survive my complicated family, it wasn't easy for me to express vulnerability to people. I still believe the only reason I was brave enough to tell Mason I loved him so early in our relationship was because the redwood trees and the Pacific Ocean flanked either side of us. It was as though those massive, ancient trees and ocean had given me strength.

One morning during Adriana's first cross-country trip, we sat outside the Green Salmon Coffee Company in Yachats, Oregon. Souvenir stores, Luna Sea Fish House, a post office, and the Pacific Ocean were across Highway 101. The ocean unraveled its glittering surface to the horizon, the sun at such an angle that it looked as if thousands of mirrors reflected its rays. The ocean breeze drifted across the highway, its salty scent mixing with the aroma from Bread & Roses Bakery. Later that afternoon, we'd buy a sourdough loaf and grill it topped with tomatoes and feta.

Adriana was perched next to me on the bench. She still had the sweet-and-sour scent of puppy breath, but it had faded to a trace. Her ears, now flaps that reached the middle of her snout, hung over her eyes like a girl's long hair. She was small enough to fit under our feet on a Southwest 737, but just barely.

Adriana was investigating a forty-pound mutt who looked like a miniature lab. Finally, after mustering enough courage, she jumped off the bench and tentatively greeted her new friend. Adriana acted confidently at home, but she was shy around strangers, a trait she'd retain into adulthood. The brown mutt was named after Princess Leia from *Star Wars*.

I talked to Leia's mom, Alice, a redheaded student at Oregon State University, while Adriana and Leia smelled each other's nether regions. Alice was studying the disappearing starfish along the Pacific Coast. I asked what exactly she meant by "disappearing starfish." She explained they were dying at an unprecedented rate due to a sickness called sea star wasting syndrome.

A middle-aged woman wearing Heidi braids leaned over from her picnic table adjacent to us and asked Alice to repeat herself. "I'm sorry to interrupt, but I feel like I need to hear this. The starfish are dying? Like forever?"

The aspiring marine biologist reaffirmed sea stars are completely disappearing from the Northwest coastline.

"Why don't I know about this?" I asked.

"I don't know why more people don't care," Alice said.

I tried to contemplate an ocean without starfish, but it was unthinkable: the two were synonymous, interdependent, inseparable. I'd never been in a beach town on the Atlantic or Pacific coast that didn't sell bleached-out versions for souvenirs. Movies, postcards, fliers, tourist commercials: all used the five-armed fish either as characters or advertisements. The starfishes' predicament, the sudden permanence of their departure, made me think about Annie, how one second she'd been twirling with excitement and the next she was dead. The starfishes' disappearing act was such a well-kept secret, I was sure that many people would feel as cheated as I did, as though they'd never had a chance to say goodbye.

Adriana and Leia, now wrestling, banged against my shins. Miss Annie would never have played with a mutt on the dirty pavement. Adriana was neither better nor worse, just different. She was a plump and sturdy fifteen pounds, so I never worried about a coyote or owl snatching her. She was resilient, whereas Annie had been fragile.

Ade and I shared a different emotional relationship as well. From the moment I'd met Miss Annie, I knew everything about her, as though we were pieces of the same puzzle. Adriana's personality unfolded at a slower pace. On that trip, I learned she was an observer. Mason and I often caught her intently watching a seagull fishing or a crab scuttling across sand. She could sit still so long that she often fell asleep in the middle of her observations. Miss Annie had never watched anything except for me. I admonished myself every time I made these comparisons. Although I didn't consciously acknowledge it, in these lists, Adriana always came up wanting. But who could compare? Annie and I had been like the ocean and the starfish.

Leia and Adrianna finally tired. Alice gave them each a baked sweet potato treat. The dogs chewed their cookies and then cleaned the crumbs off the other's maw, as though they'd been friends their whole lives.

"I'm sorry about the starfish," I told Alice before we parted.

That evening at low tide, Mason, Adriana, and I walked along Yachats's rocky coastline searching for starfish. We took pictures of every one we found.

* * *

Six dogs wrestled in a triangular yard the length of a football field situated behind two rows of military housing. Adriana was the smallest dog in the group. She was three months old. A Great Dane puppy called Zeus occasionally clamped onto Ade's head, as though she was a squeaky toy. Ade would squeal and dash under the picnic table, hiding behind my legs for a few seconds before she scampered into the fray again.

Mason, Adriana, and I were at Fort Campbell in Kentucky, having dinner with Silvio Dante's parents. Silvio Dante was a former foster dog, a sixty-pound hound with the gait of a walking horse. Seven of us sat on the Dalrymples' patio and feasted on fried green tomatoes, garbage bread, and sweet tea while our dogs played.

After dinner, Silvio's mother, Amy Dalrymple, said she needed to fulfill the ALS Ice Bucket Challenge. In 2014, people all over the world recorded someone dumping a bucket of iced water over their head to raise awareness for Lou Gehrig's disease. Amy's husband, John, poured the frigid water over his wife. She screamed; we laughed. Everything went as predicted until the plastic bucket slapped the concrete patio right next to where Adriana was sitting. It cracked the pavement like someone fired a gun right next to her head. She instantly turned and bolted down the middle of the yard. John, the first to react, chased her, feet blistered raw from a week of special ops training. Soon, they were both out of sight. Minutes later, Mason headed in the same direction as John. When fifteen minutes had passed and nobody returned, I realized that Adriana La Cerva had run away on the Fort Campbell military base, home of the 101st Airborne Division.

There were sightings of Adriana. Parents or children, playing in yards or playgrounds, said they saw a puppy sprinting toward Gate 3 or the

Inspector General's office or Mahaffey Middle School. We had plenty of help. Soldiers and their spouses pulled out flashlights and scoured Stryker Village, the apartment complex where Ade had disappeared. Amy Dalrymple posted Adriana's picture on Fort Campbell's Facebook pages.

At one point, tired and scared, I marched into the office of the military police and demanded that they help me. If they could find Osama bin Laden, I reasoned, then they could damn well find a puppy. They wished me luck but advised calling animal control for help. Dusk came and went. Near midnight we called off the search until dawn.

Mason and I drove the thirty-three miles home in complete silence. Lightning flashed in the distance; thunder rumbled; a late summer storm was brewing. I forced myself not to think about Adriana outside during a deluge, but her little blond body running *away* from me was stuck on repeat. Her ears—those floppy, sensitive ears, designed to lure and funnel sound waves—were so close to the ground that the crack of the bucket must have sounded as though a bomb had exploded. That's what I felt like on the ride home: like a bomb had exploded right in the middle of my life. I was too stunned to survey the damage, as though I had to pick through the rubble one piece at a time. Ade had disappeared just like Annie. She'd been playing with Zeus one minute and gone the next. *Why didn't I have her on a leash? Why didn't she run to me instead of away from me?*

Mason and I were waiting at the registration gate when the base opened. The storm we'd seen brewing five hours prior had weakened and then settled over Fort Campbell. I knew its exact location and strength because instead of sleeping I'd been tracking it on radar. By the time we arrived, rain was falling in a steady drizzle.

Meadow, Sara, and Floyd came with us to help the search. Mason and I wore headlamps, boots, and raincoats, so we were prepared for hours of walking in wet conditions. We combed locations where Adriana had been sighted the night before. We rummaged inside pavilions, and through abandoned office trailers, ditches, drainage pipes, bleachers, and sheds. Near the outermost fences we trekked back and forth, checking every storm drain along the cinder block wall. The sky lightened; the rain stopped. Grass clippings and mud covered our boots.

We were tramping though a ragweed field near Gate 3 for the second time that morning when I heard Adriana's tags jingling. I thought my mind was playing tricks at first; I'd been straining to hear that exact sound since the moment she had disappeared. Then I heard the noise again, and Adriana appeared at my feet like she'd never been gone. She didn't greet anyone or act as though hours had passed since she last saw us. She simply moved into line with the rest of her pack, as though she'd been waiting for us. She was perfectly dry. She didn't even look like she needed a bath. A surge of relief and elation coursed through my body.

After thanking everyone who'd helped search, and kissing Adriana about a thousand times, we stopped by the MP office. I wanted them to know that we'd found our puppy. One officer joked, "I'll let the President know we can call off the choppers."

Adriana slept in my lap on the drive home. I smelled her paws, pulled apart each claw, and traced the translucent moons of her nails. I checked the four oblong digital pads on the outside and ran my fingertip over the metacarpal pad shaped like an upside-down heart. I touched the pad behind her ankle, the round one she used as a break. They felt like rubber, mini shock absorbers already turning from fresh pink to a washed-out peach. Eventually, a hardened outer layer would cover each one. I combed my fingers through her short hair. I peeked inside her ear, a coral as shiny as the inside of a shell. I felt that common but impossible urge to communicate with her. I wanted to ask her where she'd been. But I'd never know, so I searched her body as though it held clues. I found none.

When Ade had been missing, I understood the depth of my feelings for her for the first time. Miss Annie had died two months earlier, but her absence still stung; the raw pain of loving anyone as much as I loved her terrified me. I had unconsciously built a filter over my emotions, as though I could cordon them off until summoned. But when Adriana was missing, I considered the possibility of never seeing her again. I felt the panicked terror of a mother with a missing infant. I would never have stopped looking for her. I realized Ade's love had been nourishing me all along, trickling through every mental obstacle I imposed. I realized it was time to say farewell to Miss Annie.

* * *

Gabriella Dante crawled under Mason's station wagon and stayed there. Thirty-five pounds and copper brown, Gabby hunkered down under the fuel tank. She peered warily at us from a bed of gravel. A bumper sticker, white typeface on an aqua background, read MY DOG IS MY CO-PILOT. The radiator on Mason's wagon had blown and the rear brakes seized at 250,000 miles. By then, the automatic windows didn't roll down and the air-conditioning didn't blow cold air, so he parked it outside the garage. He didn't have the heart to get rid of it and threatened he'd fix it up again one day. Dessie, Floyd, Sara, and Meadow all kept their distance from the new foster dog. They sniffed around the car for a few minutes, but mostly acted as though they didn't care.

Gabby's antisocial behavior didn't deter Adriana, who had recently turned four months old. Every five minutes or so, Adriana scurried under the wagon and slathered Gabby's snout with kisses, then charged back across the yard. She would look behind her, probably hoping Gabby was chasing her, and stayed a little longer each time she dove under the car. The fur on Adriana's ears had turned the color of caramel. Her ears often stuck out in opposite directions, as though she hadn't decided which way she wanted to wear them. One ear might be cocked toward a chestnut tree dropping nuts while the other dangled forward, two symmetrical organs at odds. Rarely, Ade coordinated her look and positioned both ears folded forward, spurts of harmony or accidental by-products of abandonment.

When neither dog popped their head out from the wagon for thirty minutes, I checked on them. They were still underneath it, side by side. Gabby narrowed her eyes at me in an anxious expression, which was comical juxtaposed against Ade's happy little face. Ade had started digging a hole right next to her new foster sister. Red mud covered her nose and tongue. It struck me then that Gabby didn't know about love, and Adriana had never known anything but love. Gabby had lived outside in a kennel for her entire fourteen months. Nobody had ever named her because nobody cared enough to give her one.

I liked to think about the fact that Adriana was born in a bramble bush on Sycamore Street, yet she had already hiked on the streets of downtown St. Louis and peed next to the Mississippi River. She had visited Nashville's famous honky-tonk bar Tootsies Orchid Lounge and had traveled from Cedar Hill to the Pacific Coast under our legs on a Southwest airplane. She had seen a bear, a redwood tree, a sea lion, and, most importantly, a starfish for the first and perhaps last time.

Except for the first two weeks of her life, Adriana has never known instability. She's never been hungry or unloved; she's never lived in a world where playing is a luxury that has to be learned. That thought fills me with an intense pride. Later that evening, when I looked out the window, Gabby was chasing Adriana around and around the backyard.

PART III

28

SAME STORY, DIFFERENT DOG, THREE YEARS LATER

I turned onto South Richards Street, a section of Springfield as destitute as Sycamore Street, except South Richards runs for eight blocks instead of four. It was around eight o'clock in the morning and I had just finished walking four dogs. Three slept in the backseat; Adriana snoozed on the passenger side. I was flying to Pomona, California, to start the 2017 National Hot Rod Association drag racing tour in two days. I returned to my job during the fall of 2016 because my savings account statement had revealed a paltry fifty-three dollars. Going back on the road again also meant I had to quit my volunteer work with Free Love and blogging about our foster dogs, both hard but necessary decisions.

A drizzle colored the morning gunmetal gray. I used headlights and drove slower than normal. Out of nowhere, a medium-size mutt with long copper hair and a feathered tail streaked across the road ten feet ahead of me. I slammed on the brakes. Two puppies, one with curly black hair and one with short brown hair, sprinted after her. The black puppy looked healthy. She bounced after her mother, like they were playing a game. The brown one was clearly sick. He wore the sharp hips and tucked tail of an ailing animal, one who hadn't adapted to street life. He couldn't have weighed more than eight pounds. I cursed. Someone honked. I swore again.

I was leaving home in forty-eight hours. Mason was on the road until the following week. We couldn't take care of a stray puppy. Not now. Even if I corralled the puppies, and that was a big if, I couldn't bring sick dogs home. It wasn't fair to anybody, but most importantly it wasn't fair to our pack. I couldn't risk their safety. How many times had I repeated this same argument? How many times did I lose? Not this time. I had learned my limits.

Yet I couldn't look away, either. I couldn't pretend these dogs didn't exist. The car behind me honked again. I flicked on my hazards and pulled onto the shoulder. The puppies followed their mother behind a wooden tobacco barn. A few tidier houses with mowed, uncluttered yards stood at each end of South Richards. The barn was next to one of these houses, a brick home with a chain link fence and paved driveway. A man was warming up his pick-up truck in the driveway. I pulled up next to him.

Dale was a wispy, small-boned man wearing a baseball cap and glasses. He dressed in a navy blue uniform, as though he worked at the Electrolux factory or maybe a transmission shop. His grease-stained fingernails supported my assumption his job involved machinery. I guessed his age at around fifty. Dale opened up as soon as I asked about the stray dogs. He seemed eager to share, as though he wanted someone else to care. He called the redhaired dog Maple, said her color reminded him of the maple syrup his grandfather brought home from fishing trips in Canada. Dale explained Maple showed up a few times a year. She hung around long enough to birth and nurse another litter of puppies, then disappeared for months at a time. Sometimes, he said, she was gone so long he thought she'd never come back.

"Maple won't let anybody touch her," he said. "She'll take a hot dog out of my hand, but if I reach for her she's gone."

How could I not think about Dawn? How many dogs just like her were delivering litter after litter on the streets of this small farming city? How could any one person or one organization make a dent in the problem?

"What happens to all her puppies?" I asked.

"I'd say about 90 percent don't make it. Like that one you saw. He probably won't make it another week. He was born sick."

Dale claimed he could end Maple's life with his grandfather's rifle, but said he wasn't "that kind of man." He explained that the previous winter there had been five dogs living behind his barn. The Springfield Police Department had shot most of them, but Maple had survived. I was hearing the same story about a different dog, three years after I'd first heard it from Jimmy.

"They do that a lot around here, don't they?"

"Sometimes," he answered.

* * *

After I returned from California, I drove down South Richards. Maple showed up after my third trip around the block. She was scavenging through empty food wrappers in the parking lot of a market. The puppies weren't in sight. I parked across the street. A mural of Martin Luther King Jr. decorated the storefront. Two gentlemen leaned against the painting, holding paper bags with forty-ounce bottles inside. One threw Maple a piece of his doughnut or biscuit. She ate it, then watched him expectantly, as though wishing he'd toss more.

I kept hoping one or both of the puppies would show up, like Dawn used to, as though out of nowhere. At the very least, I could take the sickly one to Dr. Dan. And if I caught the healthy one, I could call Free Love and ask Joan if she had any fosters willing to house a puppy. I had thought about nothing else for the five days I was gone. Maple swept through the parking lot once more, then trotted across the road. She checked both ways before she crossed, as adept as any human about societal rules. She walked within feet of my car, completely unaware that I was tuned into her every move.

Slowly, I opened my door and grabbed a pack of hot dogs off my front seat. She turned as my door slammed shut. We spent a minute or two summing each other up. I tore off a piece of meat and threw it at her paws. She sniffed it for less than two seconds before it disappeared. She ate a few more pieces before I stepped forward, but she moved back immediately. I tried again; she moved back farther. When I realized this wasn't going to be easy, I reached for her, gently but as though I had a chance. She turned and bolted down the street, tail flying behind her like a flag for the Stray Mutt Club. I watched her copper silhouette weave in and out of the shadows until she disappeared into the dull horizon. I went back the next day and the day after, but I never saw Maple or her puppies again.

29

MILLIE

Joan, Mason, and I stood in Millie Cleary's front yard on an August afternoon. It had been six weeks since we'd last tried to catch Dawn. At first, we'd had to wait for the mange to heal; but the recuperating Dawn had started spending less time at Bernice's house and more at Millie's. In fact, she'd spent enough time at Millie's that Millie now claimed her, and she didn't want any help from Free Love.

Millie Cleary stood on her stoop, looking down at us over the banister. She wore a muumuu, house slippers, and hot rollers. She was sixty-ish and tall and wide, with a bowlegged walk. Bernice had told us that Millie wasn't interested in our help, but we were trying to convince her anyway. We didn't have any other option.

"Does Night come into the backyard?" Mason asked. The backyard had a chain link fence and a gate, an ideal location for trapping her, if we could get Millie's permission.

"All the time," Millie said. "She barely stays at Bernice's house anymore."

A smirk played around Millie's mouth. She had all the power now that Dawn lived on her property, and she knew it. Since I'd met Millie, my interactions with her had amounted to nothing more than small talk and pleasantries. But she'd been against us from the time we showed up on Sycamore Street. I imagined she thought of us as busybody do-gooders, and in many ways she was right. We were disrupting the balance of her neighborhood, and she wasn't happy about it.

"Do you know we've been trying to catch Night for months now?" Joan asked in her sweetest southern accent.

"I know," Millie answered, as though the information was meaningless.

"You know this poor dog has lived on the streets her whole life," Joan said.

"Some dogs are born to run wild," Millie answered.

Millie hoarded a whole trove of old wives' tales she pulled out and proclaimed, as though she was Moses reciting the commandments. She was a dangerous opponent in a neighborhood where reading was a privilege and word-of-mouth was the primary source of information. Since we'd become involved, she had advised Bernice to sell the Magic 8 for twenty-five dollars apiece and warned her that if we bathed the puppies or separated them from Dawn before they were six weeks, they would die. She had been wrong on all counts, but Bernice's vulnerable personality was no match for Millie's will. If Millie said the grass was purple loud and often enough, Bernice would believe her.

At times, Bernice's vulnerability was frustrating; at others, it was endearing. I cared about Bernice, but more importantly I liked being around her. I enjoyed sitting on her porch and listening to her tell stories or even just talk about her daily routine. Somehow, she made chores as simple as scrambling eggs seem eventful.

What I liked most about being with Bernice is that she let me listen. During our gossip sessions, I never said much. I didn't have to. I could simply sit back and hear what she had to say, and that's what I did. When I first met Bernice on the greenway, I'd seen a hard-living woman with secondhand clothes. A lifetime of stereotypes had clouded my impression. Now, two months later, I considered her a friend. It was as though my psyche had to peel back the layers of poverty to find the person underneath, and I often felt ashamed about my initial judgments.

I'd only been inside Bernice's house a few times. The first time had been after an afternoon of waiting for Dawn to show up. My bladder full,

I asked if I could use their bathroom. Stepping inside their house was like walking into a cave: cool, dark, and musty. All the shades were drawn. The television screen lit the room. It was the only light on, but it was so bright it bathed the room in a neon glow. Bernice's husband, Tray, was reclining in his La-Z-Boy. Pillows propped up his bandaged foot.

Tray must have been lonely because he wanted to talk, and like Bernice, he wasn't afraid of sharing personal details. He openly chatted about his failed musical career (he played guitar) and his numerous children (ten, including three stepchildren) spread throughout the United States. Listening to Tray, I felt a keen tenderness for the Lees. Born poor and uneducated, they had never clawed their way out. What chance did they have?

I felt the same way about most of the people I met on Sycamore Street that summer. Amy Light, twentysomething, waifish with long stringy hair, lived next door. She wore cutoffs and white tank tops. Amy gave out blowjobs for a Little Caesars pizza and few grams of methamphetamine. I had assumed it was neighborhood gossip when Bernice first told me, but after a few days of watching Amy jump out of different cars carrying a large pizza box each time, I had to concede the rumors might be true. But even after I knew about Amy's occupation, I liked her. Like most people in the neighborhood, she cared about Dawn.

One afternoon, Amy hurried over to Bernice's porch and claimed that she'd locked Dawn in her garden. I doubted it, but a glimmer of hope surfaced anyway. Unfortunately, we were both right. Dawn had wandered inside a makeshift fence surrounding a few tomato plants; and Amy had shut her inside it. However, by the time we got there, Dawn was long gone. She had simply pushed over a board.

We had the same friendly relationship with a drug dealer named Andy, who lived across the street and grew pot on his roof. I saw more deals go down in the short time I spent on Sycamore Street than on an entire season of HBO's street-crime drama *The Wire*. Suburbans with spinner rims and tinted windows, rusted-out Impalas, and middle-class SUVs stopped at Andy's house at all hours of the day. Andy was pudgy, thirtysomething, and wore basketball shorts and Tennessee Titans football jerseys. He often bummed smokes off Mason and liked talking about drag racing.

There had been an incident earlier that summer when Joan parked her van in an empty lot next to Bernice's house. A patrol officer circling the block had pulled over and told her to move it. The lot was at the end of a cul-de-sac, and it had been the middle of the afternoon: not exactly prime time for crime. When Joan, who could have been the officer's grandmother, explained we were trying to rescue a dog, he asked if she wanted a ticket. If not, he said, she needed to get her van out of there. Finally, Andy interceded and told Joan to park in his front yard.

On Sycamore Street nothing was as it appeared. It was a place that flipped every cultural stereotype on its head: the good guys were the bad, and the bad were our friends. When we had first started chasing Dawn, I had no idea I'd grow to care about Bernice, Tray, Amy, Andy, and Jimmy: an illiterate, a diabetic, a prostitute, a drug dealer, and an alcoholic, respectively. But that summer they were my closest allies.

The only resident on Sycamore Street who didn't want us to succeed was Millie.

"Mama has fleas. You got any flea medication?" Millie asked.

"What does Mama weigh?" Joan answered.

I didn't know how many litters Mama had delivered, but her nipples permanently drooped. Her weight was twice what a healthy Chihuahua's should be. I imagined Millie as the kind of person who spent evenings cooking meat loaf and mashed potatoes for her dog. If she had children, a partner, or a roommate, I never saw them.

"You got any medicine for her puppies?"

"How old are they?" Joan asked.

"Four months. I only got two left from her last litter," she said. "She should be going into heat again soon though."

"I think I can manage that," Joan answered. I knew she was choking back a lecture about using Mama as a breeding factory, but she also understood the stakes of making Millie angry. I had to admire Joan's diplomatic skills. I had been silent through the whole exchange because

Millie rubbed me the wrong way. Ninety percent of the time, I was able to keep my cool in these situations, but Millie was a bully. And bullies brought out the petty in me, so I kept my mouth closed and my eyes down. Like Joan, I also understood the stakes.

"I'd take enough for three months," Millie said.

"I think I can manage that, too," Joan said.

"Then, I guess y'all can try to get Night next week," she answered.

Before I could inwardly cheer, Joan countered: "Now, Millie, we'll need some help from you, too. We'll need you to lock the gate when she's sleeping inside your yard."

There was a pause, a long pause. Then she nodded. Millie was the proverbial businesswoman. Everything held value, even a stray mutt living in her yard. She must have calculated that that much flea medication was a fair trade for simply shutting her gate. At that time, I didn't care why she said yes, because she did. After six weeks, we were back in business.

We knew our plan to catch Dawn had to be invincible. Millie might only give us one opportunity. We weren't novices anymore, and we didn't underestimate Dawn's intelligence, either. From our four prior attempts, we had learned that trying to catch her in the open didn't work. So we opted to try to collar her with the catchpole once she was drugged and locked inside the yard. We knew she was impossible to touch, so we decided to use a powerful sedative, one that needed an antidote (an intramuscular shot) within three hours.

A local vet offered to be on standby and administer the antidote, no matter what time we caught Dawn. We planned the attempt for Tuesday. We arranged last-minute details the day before. Mason packed the catchpole in the trunk; Joan delivered the flea medication, and triple-confirmed our plans with Millie. Most importantly, Millie promised she'd lock Dawn in her backyard. Once she was in, we'd feed Dawn the sedative. We didn't want her eating the drug and passing out somewhere where we couldn't find her. The whole plan hinged on Millie shutting her gate once Dawn came inside her yard.

I did chores all day because I was too excited to focus on anything else, but Millie never called. By ten that night, I fell asleep in a house that smelled like Murphy Oil Soap and Windex with my cell phone next to my ear. We didn't hear from anyone on Sycamore Street for two days. Bernice finally admitted that Millie had changed her mind. She didn't want us on her property.

* * *

We didn't see Dawn during the month of September. Bernice reported that Dawn slept on hay bedding under Millie's porch. She was close with Mama and the gray cat named Blackberry. Bernice said she laughed every time she saw the three "amigos" waltzing up and down Sycamore Street. But she never shared what we wanted to hear the most. She never said Dawn had moved back to her house.

By the end of October, Joan said Free Love had to officially suspend its efforts on Dawn. It was a moot point since Millie had already blocked our attempts, but I think Joan needed to make it official. She needed closure. She said the nonprofit had spent a thousand dollars on Dawn plus had vetted and rehomed eight of her puppies. How much more could we do? By then, I hadn't seen Dawn for two months, so I agreed with all of Joan's arguments. I, too, needed closure.

Mason agreed that Free Love had to focus on other animals, but he never said *he'd* give up. On his rare weekends off work, he'd cruise over to Sycamore Street. I pictured him riding to town, cigarette hanging from his fingertips, Dunkin' Donuts coffee steaming from the cup holder. He always carried the catchpole in the backseat and his camera on the passenger side. Occasionally, he'd report catching a glimpse of Dawn. One time, he snapped her picture.

In the photo, she stands to the far left and down the street, so it takes a minute to locate her. The slate pavement fills most of the foreground. Dead leaves and grass line both sides of the street. Naked tree branches wear the brown shades of an early winter landscape, and clouds limit the shadows. Dawn is facing forward, eyes indiscernible. Yet I can tell she's watching Mason. She looks insignificant, as though any second she could evaporate. As though she doesn't belong there.

30

HOWLING WITH DESSIE

Ten years before we met Dawn, Mason, Miss Annie, Joe, Dessie, and I were sitting on our deck in front of a steel firepit. The flames cast an orange glow for a ten-foot radius; everything outside the perimeter was pitch black. Back then, we were still new to the country and enchanted by the nighttime view. On that cool March night, stars flooded the sky. In Nashville, the city lights faded the stars to smudges; but not in Robertson County. Out here, the moon and the stars are the only lights. Occasionally, Mason and I pointed out falling stars or constellations. Mason claimed Orion's belt looked like a butterfly, and I pretended Cassiopeia was an upside-down M. The Big Dipper looked as if it was in high definition; it felt so real it seemed like it sifted stars.

Miss Annie slept by our feet on her pink blanket and Joe was in his dog bed. Dessie was closest to the fire. Her slick black nose gleamed. I'd heard the clichés about beagles before I met Dessie: "They'll put their nose to the ground and pick it up ten miles later," and "Have you ever met a beagle who didn't run away?" After living with Dessie, I finally understood what they meant. Her nose never stopped working, three hundred million scent glands sucking up as many odors as possible.

I once read that a dog can smell a teaspoon of sugar in a hundred gallons of water. I bet Dessie could locate a teaspoon in five hundred gallons. She loved swimming and made sleeping a full-time hobby, but she was never more fulfilled than when her nose skimmed the ground. Even that night, cuddled next to the fire, her nostrils were twitching. Later, I would wonder if she smelled the coyotes before she heard them.

Not many people guessed Dessie had hound dog in her DNA. Her shaggy blond fur disguised all her beagle-ness. But after taking a dip in Sulphur Fork Creek or getting a bath in the basement shower, she looked exactly like a beagle. Her soaking wet hair hugged her body in sleek sheets that revealed her square muzzle and squat frame. Her ears drooped like hoop earrings. Her rear legs, designed for chasing small game, angled inward. At night, her eyes looked ebony; during the day, they were mocha.

Suddenly, Dessie lifted her head and strained her ears forward. Her whole body tensed, then stilled as she focused on the woods. Seconds later, we heard a high-pitched wail that didn't sound like any howl I'd heard before. The sound was as dramatic as opera music, but there wasn't anything human about it. One wail turned into a series of shrill yips that crested in a falsetto howl. A rash of goose bumps scurried down my spine.

I looked at Mason, wondering if we should bolt indoors.

"Coyotes," Mason said. He held up his finger, signaling patience. As always, he was calm, confident, *cool*.

A pack of coyotes standing one hundred yards outside our firepit answered their leader with a chorus of quick, piercing cries. Dessie, overcome by her native language, lifted her muzzle into the air and howled with all her might. Her voice had a baritone timbre that made the deck vibrate. Joe and Annie watched her for a few puzzled moments before that primitive, instinctual sound gripped them, too. They threw their snouts up and joined her. The packs' competing cries melded into a collective hymn that vaporized the boundary between domestication and wildness. Joe, Annie, and Dessie, dogs who slept on a pillow-top king mattress, sang with a pack of coyotes, who had probably just finished sharing a deer carcass.

Their song filled me with such a sense of need that I couldn't help myself. I threw my head back and started howling with them. Eventually, even Mason joined in. Amazingly, no one, not the coyotes or the dogs, stopped when they heard our off-key human voices. We joined their harmony as though nothing mattered beyond our song. We communicated with a pack of canines in a language that went beyond species.

After that night, Mason and I called all the dogs on the deck once a month and howled until our vocal cords were sore. It was nice if our sessions fell on the full moon, but it wasn't necessary. It wasn't even necessary for it to be dark, because we occasionally cut loose in the middle of the day, too. I've learned coyotes howl for two different reasons: the leader is either calling the pack home or is advertising territorial boundaries. I've also learned that each howl has a distinct sound based on its meaning.

Three months after Annie died, I was folding clothes in what used to be the puppy nursery but was now Mason's office. It was early fall 2014, sometime after dark. I thought I heard a coyote howling. After a few minutes, I realized the singing wasn't a coyote at all. It was Dessie. The moon, almost full, spilled a white-blue light across the grass. The only two constellations visible were Cassiopeia and the Big Dipper. Dessie was thirteen, so she sang from a sitting position. She sang alone. I opened a window to hear her better and recognized her meaning immediately. She was calling her pack home.

31

Nineteen Puppies

On Thanksgiving weekend, we piled six dogs, our five and a foster, into a rented minivan for a two-hour road trip to Owensboro, Kentucky, Mason's hometown. Dessie was sleeping under my feet on the floorboard. She had stuck her snout under the dash until her nose disappeared into an air vent. She picked her spot specifically because of the vents. She found them even when temperatures were mild, at least by human standards. Her low tolerance for heat had to do with her woolly coat, so thick it smelled like an old shag rug. She was the last dog left in our original pack, the *d* in the *m3jd*: the last remaining member of that perfect formula I had tattooed on my arm. Joe had been gone for six months, and Annie for five. I still thought about them twenty times every day. I still saw glimpses of them in the woods and throughout the house and experienced that moment of surprise when I remembered they were gone. But I was adjusting. Life was starting to feel "normal" again.

Almost six months old, Adriana was still small enough to fit on my lap. Floyd, Sara, and Meadow shared the backseat. Melfi, our foster dog, whined in a crate from the rear. Mason and I had loaded the minivan to capacity. We packed our human necessities in one suitcase small enough to fit in an overhead bin on an airplane. Everything else was for the dogs. We had blankets, beds, towels, arthritis medicine, vitamins, a crate, rawhide chews, treats, leashes, toys, water bowls, and food.

Once we hit the interstate and Mason set the cruise control on seventy, the dogs fell asleep. I listened to music and enjoyed the warmth of Ade's little body on my legs. Mason held my hand. I remember thinking that we were okay. Life was okay. Even after the worst thing imaginable.

Bernice texted the second we crossed the Kentucky state line. Her message read, *Night had more babies. Help.*

* * *

Dawn delivered eleven puppies during the third week of November 2014. I'd read all the statistics about animal overpopulation. I knew that only one out of ten dogs actually has a home and that almost three million dogs are euthanized in the United States every year because of overcrowding in shelters. I also knew that number didn't include the Dawns of the world, the ones nobody logged on any spreadsheet. But it's a whole different experience to watch these statistics play out in real time. Witnessing the rate of reproduction in my community escalated my level of awareness to that of a tsunami. In six months, Dawn had had *nineteen* puppies. Nineteen homeless dogs.

Joan took a hard stance and told Bernice she wouldn't help the puppies unless Millie allowed us to resume our efforts at catching Dawn. Free Love wasn't budging otherwise. We didn't hear anything during that long Thanksgiving weekend. It rained every night. I lay awake listening to water pound on my mother-in-law's roof and hoped it wasn't raining two hours south. I wondered where Dawn had made her den. I wondered if her puppies were protected from the cold, wet autumn weather.

Bernice texted me a week later: *She had her babies at Sandra's. You can come over.*

I never saw Millie again, but if I had I would have gloated.

* * *

Sandra Dexter, her husband, their landlord, and I stood in the Dexters' kitchen. They lived three houses down from Bernice. Sandra was fifty-something, with wavy hair that fell to her shoulders. Gray peppered her temples. She dressed in jeans and a man's oversize flannel shirt, and she didn't wear makeup. Sandra didn't act sentimental but practical. She explained they didn't have the desire or money to care for eleven puppies. Her husband, wiry and hunched, smoked at the table and nodded every time his wife finished a sentence. At one point, Sandra said, "Y'all know that Night doesn't let anybody touch her." By then, I'd lost count of how many times I'd heard that warning.

The landlord looked like a younger version of Bernice, short with tan skin and hay-colored hair. She owned multiple properties on Sycamore Street, and knew the neighborhood, people, and animals. She wasn't surprised Millie hadn't been willing to help. At the end of our conversation, they all agreed that if Free Love took responsibility for all eleven puppies, we could use their property whenever necessary to try to catch Dawn.

* * *

A puppy suckled my thumb. Unlike the Magic 8, Dawn's second litter all looked alike. They resembled Rottweiler pups, mostly black with brown markings across the snout and legs. Two were slightly different, all black with wavier hair. They were all in the Popeye stage of development, where one eye opened, the other squinted. Dawn had made her second den under a trailer in the Dexters' backyard. The trailer had been parked behind Sandra's house for months. The bed held piles of reclaimed wood and stripped siding. Dead weeds concealed the sides. The back abutted a garden shed big enough for a lawnmower but not much else.

Mason and I had to crawl on our stomachs to reach the puppies. One by one, we pulled them out. We'd been worried some might not be alive, but all eleven squealed the second we separated them from their littermates. We lined up the puppies on a sheet. It was hard to imagine how they all fit in her stomach. Dawn couldn't have weighed more than fifty pounds.

The puppies squirmed and wiggled until they formed a mound of puppy fur. The bottom of their den, red Tennessee mud and flattened grass, was soaking wet to the touch. The fleas had been the problem for her first litter, but this time we were battling the cold. I dried off the pups with towels while Mason secured a tarp over the trailer, anchoring the edges with cinder blocks. He spread cedar chips over the bottom of their den.

At one point, a movement caught my eye. When I looked behind me, Dawn stood in a thicket of weeds six feet away. As always, I didn't see or hear her arrive, she just appeared. It was the first time I'd seen her in months, but she didn't look any different. Her teats were just as swollen, her fur just as dull. She was acting differently, though, more curious than scared. She must have seen Mason, but she didn't run. Instead, she stepped closer, cutting the distance between us in half. Her attention was centered on the eleven puppies bundled on a white sheet *outside* her den. Anticipation tingled in my stomach.

Mason had brought the catchpole as a second thought. It rested against the trailer. Quietly, ever so quietly, he reached for it. A northerly wind steadily blew across the yard, masking the sound of his movements. Could it be this easy? After all those failures, could we simply collar Dawn in Sandra's backyard almost by accident? She was so focused on her babies she didn't notice the pole he lowered over her head. She didn't notice the hope coursing through my body. She didn't seem to notice anything besides her puppies, until the slipknot caressed her ear. The moment it touched her, she spun around and disappeared into a field of ragweed, all dead and brown.

* * *

During the month of December, Dessie stopped walking with us. Her last long walk had been during our Thanksgiving trip to Owensboro, Kentucky, where we strolled along the Ohio River. Her behavior changed in other ways, too. Dessie had slept at the end of the bed for thirteen years. That December, she moved to the footstool, as though she needed space. Her breathing was labored on occasion; her snores turned even louder and were tainted with a thick, soupy sound. She spent most of those cold winter days sleeping over the air vents, as though she couldn't get warm.

32

The Shed

One afternoon, Bernice mentioned in casual conversation that Dawn had started napping in a shed in her backyard. During the summer, the building had been crammed with junk, but recently Bernice's landlord had cleaned it out. The only thing he'd left behind was a torn-up couch. Dawn had started sleeping in the shed so often that Bernice brought her blankets and food. I realized that the shed would be the perfect place to trap Dawn. And the more I thought about it, the more excited I got. It was exactly what we needed to catch her: an enclosed space *with walls and a door*. If we shut her inside, how could she possibly escape?

The shed was large enough to hold a car, but the back half of the floor had rotted away. Rusted coffee cans, nails, hammers, screws, and dust rags cluttered the remaining shelves. We pushed the couch to the middle and used it as a barrier so the puppies wouldn't rummage around the rotting planks. At one month, their balance still limited their mobility; before long, however, they'd be steady and would roam. We swept the floor, spread hay, filled Dawn's bowls, and plumped up her bedding. We propped open the doors, which were designed like traditional barn doors, with bricks.

Mason and I moved the puppies to the shed a few days before Christmas. Two hundred yards separated it from the trailer. We were worried about Dawn finding her pups, but we would never have a better chance of catching her. After several phone calls to Joan, we'd decided to take the risk. If Dawn didn't find them after a few hours, we would move them back.

I thought about the first time I'd seen Dawn running across Bernice's yard. Since then, I had never touched her or spent any significant time with her, but she occupied a space in my life as weighty as any friend or relative. Six months ago, I had believed capturing a stray mutt would be easy, but I had learned so much since I made that promise to Bernice. I had learned that rescuing dogs in the rural South requires a certain type of compassion, the kind of tough love that Joan possessed. She knows how to balance her emotions with common sense, and that's why her nonprofit saves dog after dog every year. That balance between toughness and love is a careful but crucial one. I had learned (in the worst way imaginable) that there is such a thing as doing too much good. While we were waiting for Dawn to find her litter in that shed, catching her felt like the most important thing in my life, and it had been a long time since I had felt that strongly about anything.

It took three hours for Dawn to find her puppies. Well after dark, Bernice texted. *She back there with her babies.*

An alarm jolted us awake at 3 a.m. Clouds veiled the moon and stars. Our thermometer read twenty-four degrees. We dressed in dark jeans and sweatshirts, clothes as black as the sky outside our windows. We swiped hunters' earthy wipes over our bodies to disguise our scent. That afternoon, Mason had raked the dead leaves in Bernice's yard so Dawn wouldn't hear our steps. We were taking every precaution. We had learned the hard way that underestimating Dawn meant failure.

Mason and I drove to Sycamore Street in silence. Thoughts of Dawn overwhelmed both of us: *Would we catch her this time? Would we fail again? If we couldn't catch her in a shed, would we ever do it?* Our plan was simple: lock her in the barn while she slept and collar her with the catchpole at daybreak, when there would be at least some natural light in that dark shed.

I dropped Mace off at the bottom of Sycamore Street and slowly circled the block. The sky spat snow, the pin-size pellets melting on the windshield. The smell of the precipitation was exhilarating, and I cracked the car window so I could breathe it in. Several Christmas trees glittered through picture windows. Colorful bulbs outlined roofs, mailboxes, and shrubs, and glowed with a magnified brightness. At night, with the festive lighting, Sycamore Street looked like any other neighborhood. It was the kind of night when anything was possible, even catching Dawn. My phone rang minutes later.

"I got her," Mason said.

"What?"

"She's in there," he repeated.

"You saw her? You're sure?"

"I'm sure," he said.

On the way home, I made Mason repeat what had happened over and over. He said it was easy. He'd shined his headlamp into her eyes before he had closed and bolted the doors. We bumped fists. I cried. He cried. I texted Bernice and arranged to meet Joan at daybreak to collar her.

Bernice called one hour later. "She ain't in the shed. She's on my porch."

33

CATCHING DAWN

Christmas Eve, 3 a.m., our alarm woke us. Mason and I repeated the steps from three days earlier. We dressed in dark clothes, swiped them with hunters' wipes, and drove to Sycamore Street in a silence weighty with thoughts of Dawn. The odds of our success had plummeted since our last attempt. Dawn was a savvy dog, and most dogs are keen timekeepers. She might remember being locked up and stay away during the early hours of the day. Bernice had watched her go into the barn the previous evening, but that didn't mean she was still there, and our success depended on it.

We rode through streets that were empty and still. A steady mist smeared the Christmas lights across the windshield. The weather was eerily similar to the last time. The temperature teetered at freezing, and ice was forming on puddles. It was the kind of morning that kept both humans and dogs in bed for an extra hour or two.

I dropped Mason off at the bottom of Sycamore Street and drove at a snail's pace around the same block I'd driven three days earlier. During those seventy-two hours, we had made some adjustments. Mason had inspected the shed and had discovered a loose board that Dawn had pried open and squeezed out through. He had nailed it closed and had then scrutinized the walls for other weak spots. The other difference was that

Joan was on standby. We were going to collar Dawn immediately instead of waiting for daybreak. Mason would have to trap her in a dark shed, but we weren't giving her the opportunity to find another weak spot. With every failed attempt, we learned something new, and we'd failed enough to write a *Catching Stray Dogs for Dummies* book.

Mason texted: *She's in there. I locked the doors.*

A light bulb hung outside the shed and radiated a feeble glow. Joan backed her van as deep into Bernice's yard as she could without getting stuck. The van was eight feet away from the door. I pulled up next to it and turned on the high beams. The lights washed out the barn in a blaring whiteness, as though it was a crime scene.

Dawn realized her predicament because she whimpered behind the doors. I heard her nervous, birdlike footsteps pacing back and forth. We'd never witnessed Dawn acting aggressively, but we'd never backed her into a corner, either. We all knew the dangers of getting too close to a frightened dog.

"Are you sure you want to go in there?" I asked.

Mason answered with a confident smile, but I noticed the slightest waver. I was the only person in the world who would have discerned this, and it was only because I knew him so well. At that exact moment, he never seemed braver to me. He flicked on his headlamp and grabbed the catchpole. His shadow loomed over the shed moments before the darkness inside swallowed him whole.

Joan slammed the door shut behind him. I blocked the entrance with wire fencing as an extra line of defense. I thought about the feat Mason was undertaking. It was going to require both grace and brute strength. Wearing only a headlamp, he was trying to collar a feral black dog in a dark shed, while puppies were sleeping somewhere under his feet. It would bother him more if he hurt one of those pups than if Dawn bit him. Nothing about catching Dawn was ever easy.

For ten minutes, we listened to cursing, growling, whining, and barking. Mason swore a lot, and whenever he yelled *Fuck!* I looked at Joan. Every time we heard a bang, I cringed. And there was a lot of banging.

Finally, Mason yelled, "Open up."

We swung open the doors and the headlights beamed on Dawn's body, as though she was on stage. Mason held the catchpole at its full length. Dawn writhed, whipped her head from side to side, and bared her teeth. Her canines glared so white the color seemed neon, as though the enamel was lit from the inside. Blood dripped down her snout and splattered on her paw. She looked vicious. In fact, the whole act looked so vicious it was hard to remember we were doing something good. Dawn struggled the entire eight feet Mason dragged her. Why wasn't there an easier way? Why couldn't I communicate our desire to help her?

Once he got her inside the cage, Dawn instantly stopped fighting. She tucked her body into itself and became as small as possible. When we lifted the crate into the back of the van, she didn't nip or bite at us through the fencing. She stared with eyes that radiated fear.

"The blood—" I said. "Did she bite you?"

"She bit the catchpole, not me. She probably cut her tongue," Mason said. "Dawn never tried to bite me."

I don't think Mason consciously called her Dawn. To everyone outside Sycamore Street, she'd been Dawn from the moment we gave the Magic 8 a bath. But hearing Mason say her name outside that shed meant Dawn was leaving Sycamore Street and never going back. She was never delivering another litter, and she wasn't going to get shot in a field behind a halfway house. We broke the cycle. Joan, Mason, and I hugged, cried, and hugged some more.

I posted our success on my blog later that day. After six months and nineteen puppies, we'd caught Dawn. A silent collective roar echoed in cyberspace from everybody involved or interested in her story. Friends texted or called and readers emailed their congratulations. My best friend sent us a bottle of champagne. I woke up on Christmas morning thinking Dawn had slept in a house for the first time in her life. It was the perfect gift.

34

BECOMING DAWN

Dawn and I stared at each other through the bars of a four-foot-by-eight-foot pen. Her honey-brown eyes glistened. I was finally close enough to see their color. They didn't hold the same hectic terror as they did outside the shed two mornings previously, but wariness persisted. Who could blame her? I tried imagining how she was processing the dramatic change in her living circumstances. Fifty hours ago, she had been roaming on Sycamore Street. Now she was trapped in our basement. She must have felt like a hostage, as though she'd been kidnapped. She was right, in a way. We *had* kidnapped her.

Mason had split our basement in half with a wall of plywood. Dawn lived in one half in her kennel. We tried making her space as pleasant as possible. My iPod played from Mason's worktable, shuffling through songs by artists ranging from Biggie Smalls to James Taylor. A lavender candle burned from the top of the dryer. It almost disguised the smell of Dawn's waste. In retrospect, we could have done without the kennel, but we were paranoid about her escaping. She had eluded us for so long that her capture seemed fragile, breakable.

Dawn lived alone in her crate. The puppies had gone into a different foster home the day after Christmas because the vet said her milk needed to dry up before he fixed her. Instead of all eleven puppies, we fostered one. I called him Tony Soprano in honor of Dawn's last litter. Tony had a wavy black coat and a bold disposition. I heard the drumming of his tiny paws across the hardwood floor. He was playing upstairs with his half sister, Adriana. I hoped Dawn heard the same drumming. I hoped the sound communicated everything I couldn't. *Tony's happy. He's healthy. All his needs are satisfied. There's no reason for you to be afraid anymore.*

Several times each day, I would find Mason in Dawn's pen. He would sit next to her on the concrete floor, two feet separating them, and read the news or scroll through pictures of race cars on Instagram. He never tried touching Dawn, but just patiently sat there. And his diligence worked, because they were developing a relationship. Before, Dawn had bolted every time he showed up on Sycamore Street. Now he was her closest friend. She would gaze at him from a safe distance with an expression I can only describe as terrified adoration, as though she didn't know whether he was real or not.

I unlatched the kennel door and stepped inside. I moved slowly, mindfully acting confident, even though I didn't feel certain. In some ways, I didn't trust Dawn as much as she didn't trust me. And I still wasn't completely positive she wasn't aggressive. She observed me from the farthest corner, but I didn't approach her. She acted so timid that I squatted, so that we were the same height. But she remained as remote as a statue. Her eyes were the only body part that moved. They followed me as I scooped her waste, mopped the floor, refreshed her water bowl, mixed deworming medicine with her food, and exchanged old bedding for new blankets. They followed me as I re-latched the kennel gate and silently said goodnight.

* * *

Dawn got spayed on January 6, 2015, six months after we first saw her on Sycamore Street. A week later Mason attached one leash to her collar and a second tether to her harness. He was bringing her inside our house for the first time. The harness was an extra line of defense in case she weaseled out of her collar. She'd been living inside our basement for three weeks. Although we had worked with her every day and saw progress, we still treated her as though any minute she might escape.

Dawn paused at the porch's steps. I thought about when we'd tried trapping her on Bernice's stoop and she'd shied away from the staircase. Mason gently tugged her tether. She looked up at him with a timid stare, then traversed the two steps quickly, as though she didn't want to dally on the ominous platforms. She'd already come so far. Dawn still suffered from the canine equivalent of PTSD, but we were working on it. The important thing was that we had stopped the cycle. Dawn would never produce another generation of dogs who would die on the streets. I'd kept my promise to Bernice.

As soon as Dawn stepped inside, we knew our intuitions had been right. She'd never been in a house before. Mason unhooked her leashes, and she immediately planted herself behind a white leather armchair. Tony, who had been without his mother for weeks, and Adriana, who loved all dogs, attacked her with boisterous affection. I had multiple people ask if I thought Adriana remembered her mother. I didn't have an answer then, and I still don't. On the other hand, I had no doubt that Tony remembered her. He hopped at her snout and slathered her with kisses. He nuzzled for her teat, but there wasn't any milk left, and I felt a keen sense of satisfaction that he came up empty. Her nursing days were over.

The other dogs must have recognized her scent from the basement because they investigated with a few sniffs of her rump, then returned to their napping positions on the floor or the couch, as though she was old news. Tony soon grew bored with his mother's stoic demeanor and pounced after Adriana. A wrestling match ensued. Mason and I went about our daily chores. Dawn occasionally peeked around the edge of the chair, but she jerked back, as though stung, whenever I caught her eye. Despite her cautious behavior, she looked good. She looked *healthy*. Her teats had visibly shrunk. Her coal black fur had turned from dull to glistening.

Throughout the day, household sounds most of us take for granted or hear as background noise alarmed Dawn. She flinched when the ceiling fan swirled on, the refrigerator opened, the screen door slammed, the dishwasher filled with water, or a chair squeaked across hardwood. When I turned on the television, she jumped; the vacuum caused a wave of shivers. Every time she felt uneasy, she looked at Dessie or Floyd or Meadow and watched their reaction. Each time they treated something as normal, each time they *didn't* react, she returned to her watchful pose. Just as Joe had always taught our younger dogs about house rules, they were showing Dawn how to act like a domesticated animal.

She also imitated them later that night at dinner. We fed the dogs twice a day, breakfast and dinner. That evening, like every other, I passed out the food bowls in order of pack rank, starting with Dessie. Dawn received her bowl last. She didn't scoot away or flinch when I placed the food by her paws. She scrutinized the other dogs eating their dinner and observed the way each mutt respected the other's space. She sniffed the food, then picked up a piece and ate it. Her bowl was empty five minutes later.

After dinner, she watched me pass out biscuits. She studied each dog accepting their treat without jockeying for more or stealing their neighbor's. When it was her turn, I squatted. Her lashes were short and blunt, too short to shade her brown eyes. I extended my gift. A few unsure seconds passed before she gently, ever so gently, in that birdlike way of hers, removed the cookie from my fingers. Inside, I cheered, but on the outside I acted as though I expected nothing less. Every small step we made with Dawn was significant.

Over the course of the next several months, our pack would continue to domesticate Dawn. She imitated their mood and behavior in every situation. They would coach her in simple things, like napping in warm laundry, ignoring the vacuum (which ran several times a day because of the monumental amount of dog hair in our house), and howling with the coyotes. They instructed her on the harder lessons, such as how to walk on a leash, respect the cats, or sit patiently on Chipotle's concrete patio while we ate our burrito bowls. They would also teach her about the benefits of running errands, because the bank's drive-through meant dog treats and so did a waltz around Tractor Supply Company. What would have taken us years to teach her, she learned from them in days.

After dinner, the pack started making their way to the backyard. One by one they exited through the doggie door. Dawn watched them stick their snouts through the plastic flap, then disappear. She listened to the covering slap shut and to the sound of their paws stomping down the stairs. Finally, she followed. I was in the kitchen rinsing out dog bowls, so I didn't see her go through the door, but I heard her. Her tags jingled as she tentatively moved down the steps. I noticed the sound because it was so new. Dawn had only lived in our house for a day, but she was already creating her own music.

* * *

Two months after Dawn had been living with us, she sat next to the kitchen door and patiently waited for me to attach her leash. She acted a little jittery when I pulled out the red vest, wrapped it around her rib cage, and snapped the plastic buckle, but it was the first time she had ever worn working gear. Dawn followed me to the car with a wagging tail, effortlessly hopping into the backseat. She wiggled herself into a spot between Meadow and Adriana. They sniffed the red vest for a second, as though acknowledging her new attire. Then, they stuck their sweating noses against the window, adding to the slobbery art already smearing the glass. We were going to the Springfield Greenway for our morning four-mile walk.

Dawn displayed perfect manners on the greenway, moving beside Adriana with enough slack in her leash to form a J. Adriana, eight months old, occasionally found a stick or chestnut and tempted her mother to play. Inevitably, Dawn caved. I allowed a tethered wrestling match to break out, but the game didn't last longer than a minute. There were too many smells on the greenway for any one thing to keep their interest for long. Driving home, I looked in the rearview mirror and saw Dawn's silhouette curled up on the backseat. Her fur was so dark it was impossible to pick out any one feature, yet her body exuded peace.

Dawn was learning quickly, but she hadn't been perfect in those first couple of months. She chewed up two pairs of running shoes, ripped the stuffing out of toys within minutes, and barked anxiously for her food bowl. She often ignored our commands when we called her name or signaled for her to sit. She also still remained timid around most humans. She had come so far that I had no doubt Dawn could overcome her remaining fears with a patient master. The problem was finding that perfect person.

After our walk, I unhooked Dawn's working gear. She seemed extraordinarily happy to have it off. I told myself she couldn't possibly know what it said. I threw the bright red vest in the trunk. It read, ADOPT ME.

35

Doing the Right Thing

I anxiously watched our country road. The sun blared through the naked branches. The temperature was frigid. Across the street, weeds billowed in the northerly wind. It was late winter. I rubbed my clammy palms down my blue jeans and wished the next hour was already over. If any of the dogs recognized my anxiety, they didn't give any indication. They acted as though it was any other day.

Dawn napped on the chaise portion of our leather sectional sofa. She rested in a place we called her spot because she slept there at night and lounged there during the day. It used to be Joe's favorite location, too, mainly because he could keep his eye on things through the picture window. I imagined Dawn did the same. Our sectional had seen better days, and the chaise portion was the shabbiest. The leather had cracked so often it split apart in large swaths that revealed more hide than leather. I threatened to get a new one weekly, but I never did, mainly because I still found strands of Joe's hair tucked between the cracks.

Finally, Mason and Bernice pulled into the driveway. Mason had gone to pick Bernice up since she couldn't drive. She was coming over to visit Dawn, to ask if she could adopt her. Bernice had been reaching out weekly to find out when Dawn was coming home to Sycamore Street. I needed to tell her she wasn't ever coming back. I suddenly wanted Mason or Joan to tell her. They had offered, but I felt I owed Bernice a face-to-face explanation. I told myself she'd understand when she saw how good Dawn looked, how healthy. But in the next second I knew that wasn't true. She would never understand.

Bernice walked through our front door wearing a camouflage jacket, sweatpants, and sandals with white cotton socks. She smelled like cigarette smoke and dusty knickknacks. On clear days, like that one, the sun reflected off our hardwood floors. In the warm yellow light, it struck me that Bernice may have been pretty once. She looked smaller and more vulnerable in our home than on Sycamore Street. The bulk of her jacket, puffy with fleece lining, swallowed her to the neck. I remembered the stories she told me about her mother's cruelty, how she'd been cleaning house and taking care of siblings since she was six, and how she'd quit school when she was twelve. I felt a surge of protectiveness, followed by a wave of guilt. This time, I was the one who was going to hurt her.

"Is that Night?" Bernice asked. Amazement tinged her voice.

Even with all that guilt weighing me down, I managed to feel a sense of pride. "That's her."

Bernice abruptly reached for her. Dawn scrammed off the couch. Bernice's smile faltered. Wanting to make her feel better, I showed her how to approach Dawn by slowly reaching under her chin. After a few minutes, Dawn allowed Bernice to sit next to her. After a few more, she allowed her to rub her fur. Bernice beamed as though she was touching her grandchild.

"When's she coming home?" Bernice said.

If I followed Joan's advice to always put the dog first, then the answer was obvious. Yet, Bernice loved Dawn, and that complicated things. How could I tell her Sycamore Street wasn't good enough anymore? How could I tell her we had plans for Dawn that didn't include a wooden shed or rotting porch? That those plans didn't include her? We envisioned Dawn's future with plush dog beds, comfortable couches, and a fenced yard. We wanted someone who could afford monthly flea and heartworm medication. Someone who walked her. Every. Single. Day.

We locked eyes. All the words I didn't know how to say clogged in my throat. Bernice's already wrinkled forehead creased even deeper. Her baby blue eyes widened and brimmed with tears. I looked away because I couldn't face her pain, a pain I caused. She knew. She had always known. Maybe that's why she had listened to Millie so easily. Some part of her understood that catching Dawn meant losing her, too. I thought about her sad-looking house, her husband dying of diabetes, and about how I was taking away an animal she loved in the only way she could, and it still wasn't good enough. Sometimes, doing the right thing didn't feel right.

"I'm sorry," I said. And I meant it.

36

DESSIE'S ELEGANT ENDING

I didn't sleep the night before Dessie died. Dr. Dan was coming the next morning to euthanize her. Dessie had lost so much weight over the spring and summer of 2015 that I could feel her ribs. Her nose, that super sniffer, was always dry, and her fur smelled mustier than ever, probably because I hadn't given her a bath for two weeks. At that point, why make her do anything she didn't want to? Her smell, that musty, earthy scent, covered every surface of our house, until it was inescapable. It was impossible to believe it would be gone in the morning. There were times that night when I thought she was actively dying, because her breathing became so labored the only diagnosis seemed to be a heart attack. I got through those attacks by reminding myself that, tomorrow, she wouldn't feel pain anymore. At one point, we were so sure she was dying that Mason cut off a piece of her hair matted into a dreadlock behind her ear. Mason could handle the reminders. For me, especially in the early days, they felt like physical blows.

Dessie had stopped eating, or we would have cooked her a special dinner, like we did for Joe. When Joe had first showed symptoms of his autoimmune disease, we spent thousands of dollars consulting specialists. They gave him numerous tests and prescribed too many pills, including steroids that changed his behavior. But he never got better, not really, and we had wondered if we were keeping him alive for his sake or for ours. We tried a different route with Dessie. Dr. Dan helped us manage any pain, but we didn't seek out specialists. Instead of doctors, tests, and pills, we gave her love.

Thirty minutes before Dr. Dan arrived, I sung out, "I love you, Dessie."

She lay on a quilt in the living room. Her snout rested on the rim of the water bowl. She lifted her front paw, as though she was telling me she understood, and I really wanted to believe she did. Her shaggy coat hung limp, but oddly enough she looked happy. Her eyes, clouded with cataracts, shone with an unnatural brightness. A few minutes later, Dessie's body started jerking. She wasn't waiting for Dr. Dan. Mason and I kneeled on the floor. We touched her everywhere because we wanted her to smell and feel us until the last second. Then she was gone: fourteen years over in seconds.

There's nothing beautiful about death, but there was something elegant in the way Dessie left us. She picked her own ending.

37

THE ASHES

Miss Annie's ashes sit between Joe's and Dessie's on my bookshelf. Annie's box is the lightest, as though there's nothing inside except for air. We didn't choose any of the containers. We let the crematorium decide. Those details never seemed important. What did it matter at that point?

Mason placed a picture behind each box. In Joe's photo, he's still a puppy; he wears paws too large for his spindly legs and unruly whiskers around his ears and snout. Miss Annie's picture is a close-up of her face. She's gazing straight into the camera with her head tilted to the side. I like to imagine it captures one of those daily moments when she was checking in on me, when we were checking in on each other. In Dessie's snapshot, she's under my feet at the kitchen table with her head resting on a chair rung. The print is black and white, but even with all the shades of gray, her slick nose, that super nose, stands out as the darkest spot in the photo.

My husband calls Miss Annie, Joe Poop, and Dessie our starter pack. I call them my first family. Now, those three unremarkable containers hold the only physical evidence we have of animals we loved for sixteen years, animals whose initials I had tattooed on my shoulder. They died with the same frequency we adopted them, one after the other, three in thirteen months. I don't know if losing them so quickly made saying goodbye easier or harder. I know I carry around three hollow spaces that will never be full again. And sometimes those empty places still ache.

When we knew Joe wasn't getting better, I had questioned whether my family would ever be the same and whether I'd ever feel that sort of love again. I've learned the answer is no to the former, and yes to the latter. I may have lost one family, but I discovered another. If canines were superheroes or heroines, their primary power would be their unconditional love, a love so powerful and pure it can heal emotionally broken people. I know because it healed me at some of the lowest points of my life. It healed me when the worst thing imaginable happened. And in the two years we fostered dogs, I watched it heal others time and time again.

The boxes rest on the fourth shelf from the bottom. When I'm working from my desk, they sit over my right shoulder, the shoulder with my tattoo. It seems odd that my tattoo is still here and my dogs aren't. It gives the fading initials a value the artwork doesn't deserve. Over the past thousand days, I'd learned grief is a permanent absence. It's a constant nagging suspicion something's misplaced or left behind. Time is the only remedy, and it still doesn't erase their absence. It only softens it. I glance at those boxes once a day. They are reassurances that I didn't imagine the love we shared. Sometimes, when I need a dose of inspiration, I'll take a second look. I've thought about spreading the dogs' ashes somewhere in the yard or the woods. But as much as they loved being outside, they loved being with us more.

38

Dawn, Three-Time Foster-Failure

Dawn approached Mason with a shy, swaying behind. Her tail slowly swished back and forth. They were on the porch. He had just gotten home from Dunkin' Donuts and held a large Styrofoam coffee cup. The aroma filtered through the screen door and overpowered the vanilla-scented candle burning on the kitchen table. The way the sun slanted across the grass, the way the katydids and evening peepers chirped from the tree line, reminded me of that day Joe ate strawberries in the sunshine. It seemed like years ago instead of fifteen months.

Dawn had been sunbathing with the other dogs. Her jet-black fur glistened, as though the sunrays released the oils in her sleek coat. I stood inside the kitchen door; if they knew that I was watching them, they didn't acknowledge me. Mason kneeled so that he was at Dawn's height, his face bent over, next to her snout. His Predators baseball cap tumbled off his head. Dawn picked it up with her teeth and lifted it upward, as though she was handing it to him.

I had just gotten off the phone with Joan. She'd received a promising inquiry about Dawn. I had mixed feelings about the news. A moment ago, it would have seemed positive, but watching Mason and Dawn together soured it. Mason was the one person who had never given up on Dawn. He was the one who had entered that dark shed on a Christmas Eve morning. He was the one who had wooed her when she was imprisoned in our basement. For months after she had moved inside, he invited her onto our bed for an afternoon nap, but she always declined. Then, a few days ago, I had caught sight of her snuggled next to Mason on the bed, and it had stopped me in my tracks. She was resting her snout on his rising and falling chest. Her eyes had been open but they were calm, as calm as I'd ever seen them.

Dawn had been living with us for eight months and up for adoption for four of them. Several people had shown interest, but Mason had always found a reason for denying each one. In the beginning, I'd agreed with his vetoes. One man planned on keeping her crated for eight hours a day while he worked. Another didn't have a job. "It has to be the perfect home," Mason would say, repeating Joan's advice as if I'd never heard it before. What he really meant was that it had to be *our* home.

I opened the screen door. "We got an email about Dawn," I said. "This one sounds ideal."

Helen Oates was semiretired but active. She had another rescue dog named Boone, whom she treated like a child. She worked part time at a health-food store and planned on taking both dogs into work with her. "Helen wants to arrange a meet and greet. When do you want to schedule it?"

Mason was as quiet as Dawn. I knew what he wanted, but I wasn't giving in. I had my mind settled on four dogs. Four would be the perfect number for us. It would be like the old days, when our entire family fit in *one* car; when each of us could walk two dogs, a leash in each hand. Besides, we'd already failed with Meadow and Adriana. I wasn't going to be a three-time foster-failure.

"I'm leaving this weekend for Indianapolis," he said.

"It's Monday," I answered. "Would Wednesday work?"

"What *would* work is if we paid the hundred-dollar adoption fee, and called it Christmas," he said.

Five minutes later our exchange exploded into a fight. Arguments, especially any that involved screaming, were so rare that the sunbathing dogs hightailed it from the deck into the living room. Every once in a while, Meadow peeped out the door, then tiptoed back inside, as though she was reporting to the pack. That fight didn't end with an agreement or a compromise. It ended with Mason whipping his coffee cup across the deck. It's a unique occasion when my cool, laid-back husband does something as dramatic as throw a tantrum. It was a sure sign I was losing the argument, but I wasn't ready to admit it.

I didn't admit it throughout the afternoon, either, even though every person in our inner circle agreed with Mason. Any time I talked to Joan about Helen Oates, she reminded me to remind Mason that he could say no anytime during the adoption process. Nancy Padfield, the person responsible for naming Dawn, didn't bother answering when I said Helen spent a lot of time at home with her dogs. She simply rolled her eyes. Her daughter Charlotte outright laughed when I explained Helen would take her to work every day. When I told our house sitter Lino Chavez that Dawn might have a new home, his forehead creased: "Nooo. Meleeza. Dawn is tranquilo here."

I was starting to teeter by evening, but I still couldn't admit it. We'd met Dawn a month before we lost Joe, and she was still in our life a month after Dessie died. I didn't know what that meant, but it felt important, as though it happened for a reason, as though the universe planned it. I kept coming back to the fact that *because* Dessie died we could give another animal a home. That had always been our rule. If we had the resources, we shared them with homeless dogs. When we started fostering, our family included five mutts. *Why not end with five?* These thoughts flooded my mind for the next few hours, but I remained stubborn.

* * *

That night I switched off all the lights, flipped on the humidifier and ceiling fans, locked the doggie door, and turned the thermostat down to seventy degrees. I was emotionally exhausted. I had just finished arranging Dawn's meet and greet for Wednesday afternoon. Helen and I had spent thirty minutes on the phone. I'd shared everything from Jimmy's story to Dawn's timid nature and penchant for chewing shoes. Helen had handled the good and the bad with compassion. If all went well on Wednesday, we'd come home without Dawn. It sounded wrong saying that if all went well we'd leave her behind, but we needed to be stronger than ever before. We needed to harden our hearts in the tradition of anyone who rescues animals. Saying goodbye would only get more diffi-cult the longer we waited. Mason would forgive me.

I walked into our bedroom: hardwood floors, bamboo furniture and blinds, a dog pillow at the foot of the king-size bed. The bed took up three-quarters of the room's width. At first, when Mason had brought up replacing our queen mattress with a king, I'd been against it, thinking we'd spread out instead of cuddle. But we ended up sleeping just like we always did, in a bundle at the center, just like a pile of puppies.

I switched on the light. The loamy smell of warm dogs wafted forward. I inhaled the scent until it filled my lungs. Mason was tucked under the covers, the pink blanket pulled to his neck. Floyd, Sara, Meadow, Adriana, and Dawn were at the foot of the bed, lying next to each other, side by side, like crayons in a box. Sara and Floyd sandwiched Dawn while Adriana and Meadow bookended the pack. They had been waiting for me to assume my position before they settled in around us. They were all half asleep and lingering in that realm between dreams.

When they roused and saw me, tails started thumping. They always greeted me this way, as though I was wanted, as though every time I walked into a room was cause for celebration. I felt the warm glow of being loved for exactly who I was, ugly parts and all. I belonged with them, and they belonged with me. We needed each other. At one time, I'd been a stray, just like these dogs, but we had all survived. And being survivors bound us together in a way that was tighter than blood. I caught Dawn's eye, drowsy and peaceful. She'd experienced so much. She had lived on Sycamore Street, survived a war zone, birthed nineteen puppies. She deserved peace. She deserved stability.

"Who thinks this is the best home for Dawn?" I asked.

Five tails drummed louder and louder, until it was all I could hear: a reverberating yes.

Mason threw back the pink blanket. He was smiling with his signature confidence. He knew I'd cave. He had always known.

* * *

Dawn's before and after pictures are taped on my office wall above all the others. Her rescue will always feel like my greatest accomplishment. The before photo is the same one I'd posted multiple times on the Farnival. Dawn is ambling down Bernice's concrete walkway after eating Kibbles 'n Bits from a paper plate. Her posture is slumped. Her swollen teats weigh her down. Her body language screams defeat. Juxtaposed next to the after picture, it's hard to believe she's the same dog.

In the second picture, she's playing with Adriana in the snow. A rare snowstorm had passed over middle Tennessee and left several inches of fluffy powder on the ground. The background is so white that Dawn's black silhouette looks etched in the snow. The only shadow is the one from her body. Dawn is mid-leap, as though she's pouncing. She kicks up snow and the powder sprays around her paws and belly. Her teats are invisible and her cockeyed ears stand vertically. Her eyes glitter with playful abandonment, as though she feels safe. She's undeniably happy, like she finally knows where she belongs.

Epilogue

Sixteen paws drum on concrete. Eight ears rotate one way, then the other. Four slick noses point high and proud. It's early morning on the greenway. A smoky mist hovers over the creek bed. Songbirds, katydids, and crickets chirp from the thick foliage lining the bank. It's never quiet in the country, but it is peaceful out here with our dogs. It's a place where words are never necessary. Floyd and Sara walk on my right side, leashes slack, pace perfectly in sync. They turn eleven this year. Gray fur peppers his copper snout and her black one, but otherwise no one could guess their age. They are still inseparable.

Meadow and Adriana walk on Mason's left side. Meadow's head reaches his thigh. She's around eight years old now, but still a Daddy's girl. Any black coloring on her body has turned blond or white, but her face hasn't changed. She still wears the distinctive maw of a shepherd. The kids at the greenway call her a wolf. Adriana, thirty pounds of pure huntress, is the only dog who walks with tension in the leash because she can't finish one scent before she's sucking in another. At six, she's calming down, but she's still the puppy of our pack, spoiled rotten.

If Dawn were walking with us, she'd be on Mason's right side, matching his gait stride for stride. Occasionally, she would glance up at him in complete adoration. Dawn lived with us for four full and peaceful years, years filled with leash-free runs through the woods, hikes all over middle Tennessee, wrestling matches, road trips, and nightly snuggle sessions. She loved her pack most of all, but she also had deep affection for the couch, air conditioning, squeaky toys, and peanut butter treats. That mutt came with a lot of mysteries, but I'm positive those four years were the best of her life.

Then, on a Friday in February, she died, suddenly, without a single warning. The day before, I had walked her twice, four miles in the morning and two in the afternoon. She acted completely normal, ate both meals, drank water, played, and napped. I flew to Phoenix that night for work because I had no reason to worry or even consider worrying. Lino said she was fine on Friday morning. But when he got home that night, she started having seizures. If she had any before he arrived, I'm not sure but my guess is yes, because by the time he got her to the vet she was brain dead. Lino was beside her when she passed, and I find a lot of comfort in knowing she didn't die alone or unloved.

The shock of losing her was overwhelming for a long time. It made me question all those months we'd spent on Sycamore Street. But then I thought about the four years she spent with us, about her nineteen puppies, about Adriana. It was all worth it.

We're mid-walk now, deep into farmland. Acres and acres of corn-fields unfurl on both sides. The dogs are in full migration mode, and we move forward through space as one pack, as one family. Occasionally, ever so faintly, I hear the rhythm of Dawn's bird-like paws tapping on concrete, meshing perfectly with our own, as though she's still walking right beside us.

—*June 2020*

About the Author

MELISSA ARMSTRONG has been independently rescuing dogs for over fifteen years, and from 2013 to 2015 she fostered and trained thirty homeless dogs for a local nonprofit. She has an MFA in creative nonfiction and fiction from the Vermont College of Fine Arts, and writes about her experiences on her blog, The Farnival (thefarnival.com). She lives with her husband and four rescue dogs in rural Tennessee. She's pictured above with Adriana (photo by Mason Armstrong).

About the Publisher

LANTERN PUBLISHING & MEDIA was founded in 2020 to follow and expand on the legacy of Lantern Books—a publishing company started in 1999 on the principles of living with a greater depth and commitment to the preservation of the natural world. Like its predecessor, Lantern Publishing & Media produces books on animal advocacy, veganism, religion, social justice, and psychology and family therapy. Lantern is dedicated to printing in the United States on recycled paper and saving resources in our day-to-day operations. Our titles are also available as e-books and audiobooks.

To catch up on Lantern's publishing program, visit us at www.lanternpm.org.

facebook.com/lanternpm
twitter.com/lanternpm
instagram.com/lanternpm